Python 3.13 Crash Course: A Practical Introduction

Matt P. Handy

Contents

Introduction: Welcome to the World of Python!

Hey there, future Pythonista!

First off, thanks for picking up this book. I know there are a *ton* of resources out there for learning Python, and I really appreciate you choosing to start your journey with me. My goal with this book is simple: to get you coding in Python *fast*, without overwhelming you with unnecessary details.

Why Python? Why Now?

Maybe you're here because you've heard about Python's amazing power and versatility. Maybe you're looking to switch careers, automate some tedious tasks, or finally dive into that data science project you've been dreaming about. Whatever your reason, you've come to the right place.

Python is one of the most popular programming languages in the world, and for good reason. It's:

- **Easy to learn:** Python's syntax is designed to be clear and readable, making it a great language for beginners. Think of it like writing instructions in plain English (well, almost!).
- **Powerful and versatile:** Python can be used for everything from web development and data science to machine learning and scripting.
- **Widely used:** Companies like Google, Netflix, and Spotify rely heavily on Python, so knowing Python can open up a lot of career opportunities.
- **Backed by a huge community:** The Python community is incredibly supportive and welcoming, so you'll never be short on resources or help when you get stuck.

What You'll Learn in This Crash Course

This isn't your typical dry, academic textbook. This is a *crash course*. We're going to skip the fluff and focus on the core concepts you need to start building real-world Python programs right away.

Here's what you can expect:

- **A hands-on approach:** We'll spend most of our time writing code and working through practical examples.
- **No unnecessary jargon:** I'll explain things in plain English, without getting bogged down in technical details.
- **Real-world projects:** You'll build a simple tool and analyze data using Python, so you can see how these concepts apply to real-world problems.
- **A friendly and supportive tone:** Learning to code can be challenging, but I'm here to help you every step of the way.

My Personal Python Story (A Quick Anecdote)

I remember when I first started learning Python… I was completely overwhelmed! There were so many new concepts to grasp, and I felt like I was constantly banging my head against the wall. But I stuck with it, and eventually, things started to click.

One of the things that helped me the most was working on small, practical projects. That's why I've included two projects in this book. Building something real will not only solidify your understanding of Python, but it'll also give you a huge sense of accomplishment.

What You Need to Get Started

The good news is that you don't need any prior programming experience to use this book. All you need is:

- A computer (Windows, macOS, or Linux)
- An internet connection (for downloading Python and a code editor)
- A willingness to learn!

Let's Get Started!

I'm excited to embark on this Python journey with you. So, fire up your computer, grab a cup of coffee (or tea!), and let's dive in! In the next chapter, we'll set up your Python environment and write your first Python program.

See you there!

Chapter 1: Setting Up Your Python Environment

Alright, let's get our hands dirty! Before you can start writing awesome Python code, you need to set up your development environment. Think of this as building your workshop before you start crafting. It's not the most exciting part, but it's essential for a smooth and productive coding experience. Don't worry; I'll guide you through each step.

1.1: Unveiling Python: More Than Just a Programming Language

So, you're embarking on your Python journey – fantastic! But before we jump into setting up your environment, let's really understand *what* Python is and why it has become such a dominant force in the programming world. It's more than just a language; it's an ecosystem, a philosophy, and a powerful tool for tackling a wide range of problems.

Python, at its core, is a high-level, interpreted programming language. "High-level" means that it's designed to be easy for humans to read and write, abstracting away many of the complexities of the underlying hardware. Think of it as using a map to navigate a city instead of memorizing every single street corner and turn. Python handles the "low-level" details, allowing you to focus on the "big picture" – the logic and functionality of your program.

Now, "interpreted" means that Python code is executed line by line by an interpreter, rather than being compiled into machine code all at once. This gives Python a flexibility that some compiled languages lack, making it easier to develop and debug. You can make changes to your code and see the results immediately, without having to go through a lengthy compilation process.

What truly sets Python apart, in my opinion, is its commitment to readability. The language's syntax is designed to be clear, concise, and almost English-like. This "executable pseudo-code" approach makes it easier to understand not only your own code but also code written by others. This emphasis on readability is codified in "The Zen of Python," a set of principles that guide the language's design. You can see these principles yourself by typing import this into the Python interpreter.

Why Choose Python? A Few Compelling Reasons

Python's popularity isn't just based on its readability, though. It's the combination of readability, versatility, and a thriving community that makes it so compelling.

- **The Gateway Language:** If you're new to programming, Python is an excellent place to start. Its forgiving syntax and gentle learning curve will allow you to quickly grasp the fundamentals of programming without getting bogged down in technical details.
- **The Versatile Workhorse:** Python's extensive standard library and vast ecosystem of third-party packages make it suitable for a wide range of tasks. From web development (using frameworks like Django and Flask) to data science (with libraries like NumPy and Pandas) to machine learning (with TensorFlow and PyTorch), Python can handle it all.
- **The Career Booster:** Python is in high demand in the job market. Companies of all sizes are looking for Python developers, data scientists, and engineers who can leverage Python's power to build innovative solutions.

A Practical Example (Because Talk is Cheap!)

Let's say you want to calculate the average of a list of numbers. Here's how you would do it in Python:

```python
numbers = [10, 20, 30, 40, 50]
total = sum(numbers)  # Calculate the sum of the numbers
count = len(numbers)  # Get the number of elements in the list
average = total / count #calculate the average
print(f"The average is: {average}")
```

This code is clear, concise, and easy to understand. You can copy and paste it into your Python interpreter and run it immediately. The sum() and len() functions are built-in Python functions that make this task even easier.

In Summary...

Python is more than just a programming language; it's a gateway to a world of possibilities. Its readability, versatility, and supportive community make it an excellent choice for both beginners and experienced programmers alike. As you continue through this crash course, you'll discover just how powerful and enjoyable Python can be. So, let's get that environment set up, and let the coding begin!

1.2: Installing Python 3.13: Setting Up Your Foundation

Now that you understand the power and versatility of Python, let's get it installed on your machine. This is a crucial step, as it sets the foundation for all your future coding adventures. Don't worry; I'll walk you through the process, step-by-step, for Windows, macOS, and Linux.

Before we begin, a word of caution: it's essential to install Python 3.13 *correctly*. A smooth installation will save you countless headaches down the road. So, pay attention to the details, and don't hesitate to consult the official Python documentation or search online if you encounter any issues.

The Common Thread: Downloading the Installer

Regardless of your operating system, the first step is to head over to the official Python website: https://www.python.org/downloads/. This is where you'll find the latest stable version of Python 3.13. Click on the appropriate link for your operating system to download the installer.

Installing on Windows: A Few Crucial Checks

Windows users, pay close attention to this section. The Windows installer has a few quirks that can trip up beginners.

1. **Run the installer:** Double-click the downloaded .exe file.
2. **The "Add Python 3.13 to PATH" checkbox: The Key to Success:** This is arguably the *most important* step. Make absolutely sure you check the box labeled "Add Python 3.13 to PATH". This adds Python to your system's environment variables, allowing you to run Python from the command prompt or terminal. Without this, you'll have trouble executing Python scripts. Believe me, I've seen countless beginners struggle because they missed this step!

3. **Install Now (or Customize):** For most users, the "Install Now" option is fine. However, if you want to customize the installation location or other options, you can choose "Customize installation".
4. **Complete the Installation:** Follow the on-screen instructions to complete the installation.

macOS: A Relatively Straightforward Process

Installing Python on macOS is generally more straightforward than on Windows.

1. **Run the Installer:** Double-click the downloaded .pkg file and follow the on-screen instructions.
2. **The Terminal is Your Friend:** Once the installation is complete, open the Terminal application (you can find it in Applications/Utilities).
3. **Verify with python3 --version:** Type python3 --version and press Enter. You should see "Python 3.13.x" (or a similar version number). It's crucial to use python3 because macOS often comes with an older version of Python pre-installed.

Linux: Package Managers to the Rescue (and a bit of a caveat)

Linux installation can vary depending on your distribution (e.g., Ubuntu, Fedora, Debian). However, most distributions use package managers, which make installation relatively easy.

1. **Open a Terminal:** This is your command-line interface.
2. **Update Your Package List:** The command for this varies based on your distribution. Here are a few common examples:
   o **Debian/Ubuntu:** sudo apt update
   o **Fedora:** sudo dnf update
   o **Arch Linux:** sudo pacman -Syu
3. **Install Python 3.13:** Again, the command varies. Since Python 3.13 might not be in the default repositories for all distributions yet, using a specialized repository is often the best option. The deadsnakes ppa is a common one for Ubuntu:

```
sudo add-apt-repository ppa:deadsnakes/ppa
sudo apt update
sudo apt install python3.13
```

4. **Verify Your Installation:** Type python3.13 --version and press Enter. You should see "Python 3.13.x". On some systems, you might also be able to use python3.

A Word on Virtual Environments (A Sneak Peek)

While we won't delve into virtual environments just yet (we'll cover them in detail later), it's worth mentioning that they are an *essential* part of modern Python development. Virtual environments allow you to isolate Python projects and their dependencies, preventing conflicts and ensuring that your projects are reproducible. Consider this a teaser for a topic that you'll definitely want to explore later!

Troubleshooting: Common Installation Issues

- **"Python is not recognized as an internal or external command" (Windows):** This usually means you didn't add Python to your PATH. Reinstall Python, making sure to check the "Add Python 3.13 to PATH" box.
- **"Command not found" (Linux/macOS):** Double-check that you're using the correct command (python3, python3.13) and that Python is installed correctly.
- **Permission errors:** On Linux/macOS, you might need to use sudo to run certain commands.

You've Installed Python! What's Next?

Congratulations! You've successfully installed Python 3.13 on your system. You're now one step closer to becoming a Python pro. In the next section, we'll choose and configure a code editor, which will make writing and running Python code much easier.

1.3: Your Code Editor: The Architect's Workbench

Think of your code editor as an architect's workbench. It's where you'll spend countless hours crafting your Python masterpieces. A good code editor can significantly improve your productivity, reduce errors, and make coding a more enjoyable experience.

While you *could* technically write Python code in a simple text editor like Notepad or TextEdit, you'd be missing out on a wealth of features that make a dedicated code editor indispensable. These features include syntax highlighting, code completion, debugging tools, and much more.

The choice of code editor is a personal one; there's no single "best" editor for everyone. However, I strongly recommend Visual Studio Code (VS Code) for beginners (and many experienced developers as well). It strikes a fantastic balance between simplicity, power, and extensibility.

Why I Recommend VS Code: A Personal Perspective

In my experience, VS Code is an excellent choice for Python development because it's:

- **Free and Open Source:** You can use it without paying a dime, and it's backed by a vibrant community.
- **Lightweight and Fast:** It doesn't bog down your system, even when working with large projects.
- **Highly Customizable:** You can install extensions to add support for different languages, frameworks, and tools.
- **Excellent Python Support:** The official Python extension for VS Code provides syntax highlighting, code completion, linting, debugging, and more.

Setting Up VS Code for Python: A Step-by-Step Guide

1. **Download and Install VS Code:** Head over to https://code.visualstudio.com/ and download the installer for your operating system. The installation process is straightforward; just follow the on-screen instructions.
2. **Install the Python Extension:** Once VS Code is installed, open it and click on the Extensions icon in the Activity Bar (it looks like a square with another square coming out of it). Search for "Python" by Microsoft and click "Install." This extension is essential for a seamless Python development experience.
3. **Select Your Python Interpreter:** VS Code needs to know which Python interpreter to use. It will usually detect your Python installation automatically. If you have multiple versions of Python installed, you might need to select the correct interpreter manually. To do this, press Ctrl+Shift+P (or Cmd+Shift+P on macOS) to open the Command Palette, type "Python: Select Interpreter," and choose the appropriate Python 3.13 interpreter.

4. **(Optional) Install Code Runner:** While VS Code has built-in debugging tools, the "Code Runner" extension provides a convenient way to quickly run your code without setting up a debugging configuration. Search for "Code Runner" in the Extensions Marketplace and install it.

A Quick VS Code Demo

Let's create a simple Python file and run it in VS Code.

1. **Create a new file:** In VS Code, create a new file (File -> New File).
2. **Save the file as hello.py:** It's important to save the file with the .py extension so that VS Code recognizes it as a Python file.
3. **Type the following code:**

```python
name = input("Enter your name: ")
print(f"Hello, {name}!")
```

4. **Run the code:** If you installed Code Runner, you can simply right-click in the editor and select "Run Code." Otherwise, you can use VS Code's debugging tools (which we'll cover later) or run the code from the terminal.
   If you run the code, it should ask you for your name, and print a greeting.

Beyond VS Code: Exploring Other Options

While I highly recommend VS Code, it's not the only game in town. Here are a few other popular code editors and IDEs that you might want to consider:

- **PyCharm:** A powerful IDE (Integrated Development Environment) specifically designed for Python development. It offers a wealth of features, including advanced debugging tools, code analysis, and refactoring support. PyCharm has a free Community Edition and a paid Professional Edition.
- **Sublime Text:** A lightweight and highly customizable code editor. It's known for its speed and flexibility.
- **Atom:** A free, open-source code editor developed by GitHub. It's similar to VS Code in many ways.

Ultimately, the best code editor is the one that you feel most comfortable using. I encourage you to try out a few different editors and see which one suits your workflow best.

In Conclusion: Choose Wisely, Configure Carefully

Your code editor is your primary tool for writing Python code. Take the time to choose an editor that you like and configure it properly. With the right setup, you'll be well on your way to becoming a Python coding wizard!

1.4: Hello, World! Taking Your First Steps in Python

This is it! The moment you've been waiting for. You've installed Python, you've chosen a code editor, and now it's time to write and run your very first Python program. We're going to start with the classic "Hello, World!" program, but don't let its simplicity fool you. This program is a crucial rite of passage for any aspiring programmer. It confirms that your environment is set up correctly and gives you a taste of the joy of seeing your code come to life.

Think of it as the first brick laid in the foundation of your coding empire. It's small, but incredibly significant.

Why "Hello, World!"? A Bit of History

You might be wondering why almost every programming tutorial starts with "Hello, World!". The tradition dates back to a 1974 Bell Laboratories internal memorandum by Brian Kernighan, one of the co-authors of the C programming language. The "Hello, World!" program has since become a standard way to introduce beginners to a new programming language.

Crafting Your First Python Program

1. **Open Your Code Editor:** Launch VS Code (or your preferred code editor).
2. **Create a New File:** Go to File -> New File (or press Ctrl+N or Cmd+N).
3. **Type the Code:** Type the following Python code into the file:

```
print("Hello, World!")
```

That's it! It's a single line of code, but it's packed with meaning. The print() function is a built-in Python function that displays text (or other data) on the screen. The text "Hello, World!" is a string literal, which is simply a sequence of characters enclosed in quotation marks.

4. **Save the File:** Save the file as hello.py. Make sure you save it with the .py extension. This tells your operating system and your code editor that it's a Python file. Choose a location where you can easily find it later (e.g., a "PythonProjects" folder on your desktop).

Running Your Code: Three Different Approaches

Now that you've written your code, it's time to run it. There are several ways to run Python code, and I'll show you three of the most common methods:

Method 1: Running from the Command Line (Terminal)

This method gives you a direct connection to the Python interpreter.

1. **Open a Terminal or Command Prompt:** On Windows, search for "cmd" in the Start menu. On macOS, open the Terminal application (Applications/Utilities). On Linux, you'll typically have a terminal application readily available.
2. **Navigate to the Directory:** Use the cd command (change directory) to navigate to the folder where you saved hello.py. For example, if you saved it in a folder called "PythonProjects" on your desktop, you might type:

```
cd Desktop/PythonProjects   # macOS/Linux
```

or

```
cd Desktop\PythonProjects # Windows
```

3. **Run the Program:** Type the following command and press Enter:

```
python hello.py  # Windows (if Python is in your PATH)
python3 hello.py # macOS/Linux
python3.13 hello.py #if you have multiple python versions
```

If everything is set up correctly, you should see "Hello, World!" printed on the screen.

Method 2: Running from VS Code (with Code Runner)

If you installed the Code Runner extension in VS Code (as recommended in the previous section), this is a very convenient way to run your code.

1. **Open hello.py in VS Code.**
2. **Right-Click in the Editor:** Right-click anywhere in the hello.py window.
3. **Select "Run Code":** Choose "Run Code" from the context menu.

    The output ("Hello, World!") will appear in the Output panel at the bottom of VS Code.

Method 3: Running from VS Code (Using the Terminal)

VS Code has an integrated terminal.

1. Open hello.py in VS Code
2. Press Ctrl + `` (or Cmd + ``) to open the terminal
3. Type the following command and press Enter:

```
python hello.py  # Windows (if Python is in your PATH)
python3 hello.py # macOS/Linux
python3.13 hello.py #if you have multiple python versions
```

    If everything is set up correctly, you should see "Hello, World!" printed on the screen.

Understanding What Just Happened

When you run python hello.py, you're telling the Python interpreter to execute the code in the hello.py file. The interpreter reads the code line by line, performs the actions specified (in this case, printing "Hello, World!"), and then exits.

Congratulations! You're a Python Programmer!

Okay, maybe not quite yet, but you've taken a crucial first step. You've written and run your first Python program. Take a moment to celebrate your accomplishment!

In the next section, we'll explore the Python REPL, which is an interactive environment where you can experiment with Python code in real-time.

1.5: The Python REPL: Your Interactive Playground

You've run your first Python program, which is a significant milestone! Now, let's explore another essential tool in the Python developer's arsenal: the REPL. The REPL (Read-Eval-Print Loop) is an interactive Python interpreter that provides a live, immediate environment for experimenting with code. It's like having a conversation with Python itself!

Think of the REPL as a sandbox where you can freely try out code snippets, test ideas, and explore Python's features without the need to create separate files. It's an invaluable tool for learning, debugging, and quickly verifying your understanding of Python concepts.

Why the REPL is Your Best Friend (Especially When Learning)

I consider the REPL to be one of the most powerful learning tools for Python. Here's why:

- **Immediate Feedback:** You type a line of code, press Enter, and immediately see the result. This rapid feedback loop allows you to quickly learn from your mistakes and solidify your understanding.
- **Experimentation Without Consequences:** You can try out different code snippets without worrying about breaking your program. The REPL is a safe space to explore and experiment.
- **Debugging on the Fly:** You can use the REPL to inspect variables, test functions, and track down errors in your code in real-time.
- **Discovering New Things:** The REPL encourages exploration. You can easily try out new functions, modules, and features to see how they work.

Accessing the Python REPL: A Simple Process

Getting into the REPL is incredibly easy. Just follow these steps:

1. **Open a Terminal or Command Prompt:** The same way you did when running hello.py.
2. **Type python (or python3 or python3.13) and Press Enter:**
   - **Windows:** If you added Python to your PATH during installation, simply type python and press Enter.
   - **macOS/Linux:** Type python3 (or python3.13 if you have multiple Python versions) and press Enter.

You should see the Python prompt >>>, indicating that you're now in the REPL.

A Taste of the REPL's Power: A Few Examples

Let's try out a few simple commands in the REPL:

1. **Basic Arithmetic:**

```
>>> 2 + 2
4
```

The REPL evaluates the expression 2 + 2 and prints the result 4.

2. **Variable Assignment:**

```
>>> name = "Alice"
>>> print("Hello, " + name + "!")
Hello, Alice!
```

You can assign values to variables and use them in expressions.

3. **Importing Modules:**

```
>>> import math
>>> math.sqrt(16)
4.0
```

You can import modules and use their functions.

Exploring Python Features in the REPL

The REPL is a great way to explore Python's features. For example, let's say you want to learn more about the print() function. You can use the help() function to get documentation:

```
>>> help(print)
Help on built-in function print in module builtins:

print(...)
    print(value, ..., sep=' ', end='\n', file=sys.stdout,
flush=False)

    Prints the values to a stream, or to sys.stdout by
default.
    Optional keyword arguments:
    file:   a file-like object (stream); defaults to the
current sys.stdout.
    sep:    string inserted between values, default a space.
    end:    string appended after the last value, default a
newline.
    flush:  whether to forcibly flush the stream.
```

The help() function displays the documentation for the print() function, including its arguments and behavior.

Leaving the REPL: A Simple Exit

To exit the REPL, simply type exit() and press Enter:

```
>>> exit()
```

You'll be returned to your terminal or command prompt.

Beyond the Basics: Customizing Your REPL (For Later!)

As you become more experienced with Python, you might want to customize your REPL to make it more powerful and convenient. There are several tools and libraries that can enhance the REPL, such as:

- **ipython:** An enhanced interactive Python shell with features like tab completion, syntax highlighting, and object introspection.
- **ptpython:** Another powerful REPL with advanced features like auto-completion, syntax highlighting, and a vi-style editor.

We won't cover these tools in detail in this crash course, but they are definitely worth exploring once you've mastered the basics.

The REPL: Your Constant Companion

As you continue your Python journey, remember that the REPL is your constant companion. Use it to experiment, learn, and debug your code. It's a powerful tool that will help you become a more confident and proficient Python programmer.

Chapter 2: Core Python Essentials

Welcome to Chapter 2! Now that you've got your Python environment set up, it's time to start learning the core concepts that will allow you to write real Python code. This chapter will cover variables, data types, operators, string manipulation, input/output, and the basics of Python code style. These are the fundamental building blocks you'll use to construct your Python programs.

2.1: Variables and Data Types: Where Information Lives and How Python Understands It

We've talked about setting up your environment; now it's time to delve into the heart of how Python thinks about and manipulates information. We're talking about variables and data types. It's tempting to gloss over these as "basic," but they're the bedrock of *everything* you'll do in Python. Solid understanding here means smoother sailing later on.

Variables: More Than Just Labeled Boxes

Imagine a variable not just as a box with a label, but as a pointer – a reference – to a specific place in your computer's memory. When you write x = 10, you're asking Python to:

1. Find an available spot in memory.
2. Store the value 10 in that spot.
3. Create a label, x, that *points* to that memory location.

From then on, whenever you use x in your code, Python knows to go to that memory location and retrieve the value stored there. This concept of "pointing" is fundamental to how Python (and many other languages) work.

This understanding has real implications. For example, when you reassign x = 20, Python *doesn't* modify the original value 10. Instead, it finds a *new* spot in memory, stores 20 there, and updates x to point to this new location. The old memory location might eventually be reclaimed by the system.

Dynamic Typing: Python's Flexibility and Your Responsibility

Python's dynamic typing is a double-edged sword. On the one hand, it makes coding faster and more intuitive. You don't have to declare types, so you can write code like this:

```
    x = 10
x = "Hello"
x = [1, 2, 3]
```

Python happily accepts each reassignment, changing the type of x as needed. This is incredibly convenient!

However, this convenience comes with responsibility. Because Python doesn't enforce type constraints, it's up to *you* to ensure that you're using the right types in your operations. As we saw earlier, trying to add a string and an integer directly will result in an error.

This is where good coding practices come in. Use descriptive variable names (e.g., user_age instead of just age), and be mindful of the operations you're performing. Tools like linters (which we'll discuss later) can help catch potential type errors before you even run your code.

Data Types: The Blueprint for Understanding Data

Data types define the *kind* of data a variable can hold and the operations that can be performed on that data. Python's built-in data types provide a rich set of tools for representing different kinds of information.

Let's revisit the most common data types, with a slightly different perspective:

- **int (Integers):** Represents whole numbers. Crucially, Python 3 handles integers of arbitrary size. You're not limited to a fixed number of bits. Use them for counters, quantities, and anything that can be represented as a whole number.
- **float (Floating-Point Numbers):** Represents numbers with decimal points. Use them for measurements, calculations involving fractions, and anything requiring precision. Be aware of potential floating-point inaccuracies (e.g., $0.1 + 0.2$ might not be exactly 0.3 due to how floats are stored internally).
- **str (Strings):** Represents text. Strings are immutable sequences of characters. Use them for names, messages, and any textual data.

- **bool (Booleans):** Represents truth values (True or False). Use them for logical conditions, flags, and anything that represents a yes/no state.
- **list (Lists):** Represents ordered, mutable sequences of items. Lists are incredibly versatile. Use them to store collections of related items, and remember that they can contain items of different types (although it's generally good practice to keep them homogenous).
- **tuple (Tuples):** Represents ordered, *immutable* sequences of items. Immutability can be an advantage. Use tuples when you want to ensure that a collection of items cannot be accidentally modified.
- **dict (Dictionaries):** Represents collections of key-value pairs. Dictionaries are incredibly powerful for representing structured data. Use them when you need to associate values with specific keys (e.g., a person's name with their age).

Type Hints: Bringing Structure to Dynamic Typing (A Glimpse into the Future)

While Python is dynamically typed, it *does* support type hints. Type hints allow you to optionally specify the expected data types of variables, function arguments, and return values. These hints are not enforced at runtime (by default), but they can be used by linters and other tools to help you catch type errors early.

For example:

```
    def greet(name: str) -> str:
  return f"Hello, {name}!"

greet("Alice")  # Works fine
greet(123)  # Will likely be flagged by a linter, even though
it runs
```

We'll cover type hints in more detail later, but it's worth knowing that they exist and that they can help you write more robust Python code.

A Practical Exercise: Building a Simple Inventory System

Let's put these concepts into practice. Imagine you're building a simple inventory system for a store. You might use variables and data types like this:

```
        product_name = "Laptop"  # str
product_price = 1200.00 # float
quantity_in_stock = 50  # int
is_available = True      # bool

print(f"Product: {product_name}, Price: ${product_price}, In
Stock: {quantity_in_stock}, Available: {is_available}")

# Simulate a sale
quantity_in_stock = quantity_in_stock - 1
print(f"Updated stock: {quantity_in_stock}")
```

This is a simplified example, but it demonstrates how variables and data types are used to represent real-world information in a Python program.

Key Takeaways

- Variables are more than just "boxes"; they're pointers to memory locations.
- Dynamic typing provides flexibility but requires careful attention to type safety.
- Data types define the kind of data a variable can hold and the operations that can be performed on it.
- Type hints (optional) can help you catch type errors early.
- Understanding variables and data types is fundamental to writing effective Python code.

2.2: Operators: The Verbs of the Python Language

We've established variables as the nouns of the programming world - the containers holding information. Now, let's introduce the verbs: operators. Operators are special symbols that perform operations on variables and values. They're the action words that allow you to manipulate data, make comparisons, and control the flow of your program. Without them, your variables would just sit there, doing nothing!

Think of operators as the tools in your toolbox. You have different tools for different jobs, and knowing which tool to use (and how to use it) is crucial for getting the job done right.

Arithmetic Operators: The Foundation of Calculation

These are the operators you probably learned in grade school, but they're just as important in programming:

- + (Addition): Adds two operands.
- - (Subtraction): Subtracts the second operand from the first.
- * (Multiplication): Multiplies two operands.
- / (Division): Divides the first operand by the second. *Important Note: In Python 3, division always returns a float, even if the operands are integers.*
- // (Floor Division): Divides the first operand by the second and returns the *integer* part of the result (i.e., it truncates the decimal).
- % (Modulo): Returns the remainder of the division of the first operand by the second. This is incredibly useful for tasks like determining if a number is even or odd.
- ** (Exponentiation): Raises the first operand to the power of the second.

Let's see them in action:

```
x = 10
y = 3

print(f"x + y = {x + y}")      # Output: x + y = 13
print(f"x - y = {x - y}")      # Output: x - y = 7
print(f"x * y = {x * y}")      # Output: x * y = 30
print(f"x / y = {x / y}")      # Output: x / y =
3.3333333333333335
print(f"x // y = {x // y}")   # Output: x // y = 3
print(f"x % y = {x % y}")     # Output: x % y = 1
print(f"x ** y = {x ** y}")   # Output: x ** y = 1000
```

A key thing to notice is the subtle but very important difference between / and //. This is something that can cause bugs if you aren't careful!

Comparison Operators: Asking Questions About Data

Comparison operators allow you to compare two values and determine their relationship. They always return a boolean value (True or False). These are essential for making decisions in your code (which we'll cover in the next chapter).

- == (Equal to): Returns True if the operands are equal, False otherwise.

- != (Not equal to): Returns True if the operands are not equal, False otherwise.
- > (Greater than): Returns True if the left operand is greater than the right operand, False otherwise.
- < (Less than): Returns True if the left operand is less than the right operand, False otherwise.
- >= (Greater than or equal to): Returns True if the left operand is greater than or equal to the right operand, False otherwise.
- <= (Less than or equal to): Returns True if the left operand is less than or equal to the right operand, False otherwise.

Example:

```
a = 5
b = 10

print(f"a == b: {a == b}")   # Output: a == b: False
print(f"a != b: {a != b}")   # Output: a != b: True
print(f"a > b: {a > b}")     # Output: a > b: False
print(f"a < b: {a < b}")     # Output: a < b: True
print(f"a >= b: {a >= b}")   # Output: a >= b: False
print(f"a <= b: {a <= b}")   # Output: a <= b: True
```

Logical Operators: Combining Conditions

Logical operators allow you to combine boolean expressions to create more complex conditions. They are used extensively in conditional statements and loops.

- and (Logical AND): Returns True if both operands are True, False otherwise.
- or (Logical OR): Returns True if at least one operand is True, False otherwise.
- not (Logical NOT): Returns the opposite of the operand's boolean value.

Example:

```
p = True
q = False

print(f"p and q: {p and q}")   # Output: p and q: False
print(f"p or q: {p or q}")     # Output: p or q: True
print(f"not p: {not p}")       # Output: not p: False
```

Assignment Operators: Shorthand for Common Operations

Assignment operators provide a shorthand way to perform an operation and assign the result back to the same variable.

- = (Assignment): Assigns the value on the right to the variable on the left.
- += (Add and Assign): Adds the right operand to the left operand and assigns the result to the left operand (e.g., x += 5 is equivalent to x = x + 5).
- -= (Subtract and Assign): Subtracts the right operand from the left operand and assigns the result to the left operand.
- *= (Multiply and Assign): Multiplies the left operand by the right operand and assigns the result to the left operand.
- /= (Divide and Assign): Divides the left operand by the right operand and assigns the result to the left operand.
- //= (Floor Divide and Assign): Performs floor division and assigns the result.
- %= (Modulo and Assign): Performs modulo operation and assigns the result.
- **= (Exponentiate and Assign): Raises the left operand to the power of the right operand and assigns the result.

Example:

```
x = 10

x += 5   # x is now 15
print(x)

x *= 2   # x is now 30
print(x)
```

These assignment operators can save you typing and make your code more concise.

Operator Precedence: The Order of Operations

Just like in mathematics, operators in Python have precedence. This determines the order in which they are evaluated in an expression. You can use parentheses to override the default precedence.

Here's a simplified list of operator precedence (from highest to lowest):

1. () (Parentheses)
2. ** (Exponentiation)
3. *, /, //, % (Multiplication, Division, Floor Division, Modulo)
4. +, - (Addition, Subtraction)
5. ==, !=, >, <, >=, <= (Comparison Operators)
6. not (Logical NOT)
7. and (Logical AND)
8. or (Logical OR)

When in doubt, use parentheses to make your code more readable and to ensure that expressions are evaluated in the order you intend.

A Practical Example: Calculating a Discounted Price

Let's combine several operators to calculate a discounted price:

```
original_price = 100
discount_percentage = 20
discount_amount = original_price * (discount_percentage / 100)
final_price = original_price - discount_amount

print(f"Original Price: ${original_price}")
print(f"Discount: {discount_percentage}%")
print(f"Final Price: ${final_price}")
```

In Summary: Mastering Operators is Key

Operators are the action words of the Python language. They allow you to manipulate data, make comparisons, and control the flow of your program. By mastering operators, you'll gain the power to build complex and sophisticated Python applications.

End of Section 2.2

Key Improvements:

- **Presented operators as "verbs":** Provided a more intuitive way to understand their role.
- **Explained the subtle difference between / and //:** Highlighted a common source of errors.
- **Demonstrated the use of assignment operators:** Showed how to write more concise code.
- **Explained operator precedence:** Emphasized the importance of understanding the order of operations.
- **Provided a practical example that combined several operators:** Showed how operators are used in a real-world scenario.
- **Maintained a conversational and engaging tone:** Kept the language accessible and enthusiastic.

How does this revised section feel now? Is it comprehensive and insightful? Or still more improvements needed?

2.3: String Manipulation: Taming the Textual Beast

Strings are everywhere in programming. User input, file contents, web data – it all comes down to text. So mastering string manipulation is essential for any Python programmer. Fortunately, Python provides a rich set of tools for working with strings, allowing you to extract, modify, and format text with ease.

Think of strings as sequences of characters, like beads on a string. You can access individual beads, cut the string into pieces, join strings together, and much more.

Strings are Immutable: An Important Concept

Before we dive into the tools, it's crucial to understand that strings in Python are *immutable*. This means that once you create a string, you can't change it directly. Instead, string operations create *new* strings based on the original.

This might seem limiting at first, but it has several advantages:

- **Efficiency:** Immutability allows Python to optimize string storage and operations.
- **Safety:** Immutability prevents accidental modification of strings, making your code more predictable.

So, remember: string operations always create new strings.

Slicing: Extracting Substrings

Slicing allows you to extract a portion of a string, creating a new substring. You specify the start and end indices of the desired substring:

```
text = "Python is awesome!"

print(text[0:6])  # Output: Python (Characters from index 0
up to, but not including, index 6)
print(text[7:9])  # Output: is (Characters from index 7 up
to, but not including, index 9)
print(text[10:])  # Output: awesome! (Characters from index
10 to the end of the string)
print(text[:6])   # Output: Python (Characters from the
beginning up to, but not including, index 6)
print(text[:])    # Output: Python is awesome! (A copy of the
entire string)
```

Understanding slicing is essential for extracting specific parts of a string, like a filename from a path or a specific word from a sentence.

String Methods: The Swiss Army Knife of Text Manipulation

Python provides a wealth of built-in string methods that allow you to perform a wide range of operations on strings. Here are some of the most useful ones:

- **len():** Returns the length of the string (the number of characters).

```
text = "Hello"
print(len(text))  # Output: 5
```

- **.lower():** Converts the string to lowercase.

```
text = "Hello World"
print(text.lower())  # Output: hello world
```

- **.upper():** Converts the string to uppercase.

```
text = "Hello World"
```

31

```
print(text.upper())   # Output: HELLO WORLD
```

- **.strip():** Removes leading and trailing whitespace (spaces, tabs, newlines).

```
text = "   Hello World   "
print(text.strip())   # Output: Hello World
```

- **.find():** Finds the first occurrence of a substring and returns its index. Returns -1 if the substring is not found.

```
text = "Python is awesome!"
print(text.find("is"))   # Output: 7
print(text.find("Java"))   # Output: -1
```

- **.replace():** Replaces all occurrences of a substring with another substring.

```
text = "Hello World"
print(text.replace("World", "Python"))   # Output: Hello
Python
```

- **.split():** Splits the string into a list of substrings based on a delimiter (default is whitespace).

```
text = "Python is awesome"
words = text.split()
print(words)   # Output: ['Python', 'is', 'awesome']

csv_data = "name,age,city"
fields = csv_data.split(",")
print(fields) #Output: ['name', 'age', 'city']
```

- **.join():** Joins a list of strings into a single string, using a specified delimiter.

```
words = ["Python", "is", "awesome"]
text = " ".join(words)
print(text)   # Output: Python is awesome

fields = ['name', 'age', 'city']
csv_data = ",".join(fields)
```

```
print(csv_data) #Output: name,age,city
```

This is just a small sampling of the available string methods. You can find a complete list in the Python documentation.

String Formatting: Crafting Elegant Text

String formatting allows you to create dynamic strings by inserting values into placeholders. Python offers several ways to format strings, but the most modern and recommended approach is to use f-strings (formatted string literals).

F-strings are created by prefixing a string with the letter f. You can then embed expressions inside curly braces {}. These expressions will be evaluated and their values inserted into the string.

```
name = "Alice"
age = 30

message = f"My name is {name} and I am {age} years old."
print(message)   # Output: My name is Alice and I am 30 years
old.

# You can even perform calculations inside the f-string:
price = 100
discount = 0.2
final_price = f"The final price is ${price * (1 -
discount):.2f}" # format to 2 decimals
print(final_price) #Output: The final price is $80.00
```

F-strings are incredibly powerful and readable, making them the preferred choice for string formatting in modern Python.

A Practical Example: Parsing a Log File

Let's put these skills to use with a practical example. Imagine you have a log file with lines like this:

```
2023-10-27 10:00:00 - INFO - User logged in: JohnDoe
2023-10-27 10:05:00 - WARNING - Invalid password attempt:
JaneDoe
```

```
2023-10-27 10:10:00 - ERROR - Database connection failed
```

You can use string manipulation to parse these lines and extract the date, time, log level, and message:

```python
    log_line = "2023-10-27 10:00:00 - INFO - User logged
in: JohnDoe"

parts = log_line.split(" - ")

date_time = parts[0]
log_level = parts[1]
message = parts[2]

print(f"Date/Time: {date_time}")
print(f"Log Level: {log_level}")
print(f"Message: {message}")

# Further split the date_time:
date, time = date_time.split()
print(f"Date: {date}")
print(f"Time: {time}")
```

This is a simplified example, but it demonstrates how string manipulation can be used to process real-world data.

In Summary: Strings are Your Canvas

Strings are a fundamental data type in Python, and mastering string manipulation is essential for any programmer. Use the techniques we've covered to extract, modify, and format text to your heart's content. The possibilities are endless!

2.4: Input and Output: The Bridge Between Your Program and the World

So far, we've mostly been working with data that's hardcoded into our programs. But what if you want your program to interact with the user, to get information from them and provide results back? That's where input and output (I/O) come in.

34

I/O is the bridge that connects your program to the outside world. It allows you to get data from the user (input) and display information back to them (output). Without I/O, your programs would be isolated and limited.

Output: Showing Results with print()

We've already been using the print() function to display output to the console. But let's delve a little deeper. print() takes one or more arguments, converts them to strings, and displays them on the screen, separated by spaces by default.

```
name = "Alice"
age = 30
print("Hello,", name, "! You are", age, "years old.")
```

This is perfectly fine, but using f-strings for output is generally preferred because they're more readable and flexible:

```
name = "Alice"
age = 30
print(f"Hello, {name}! You are {age} years old.")
```

The print() function also accepts optional keyword arguments to customize its behavior:

- sep: Specifies the separator between the arguments (default is a space).

  ```
  print("a", "b", "c", sep=", ")   # Output: a, b, c
  ```

- end: Specifies what to print at the end of the line (default is a newline character \n).

  ```
  print("Hello", end=" ")
  print("World")   # Output: Hello World
  ```

- file: Specifies the file to write the output to (default is sys.stdout, which is the console).

These options give you fine-grained control over how your output is formatted.

Input: Getting Information with input()

The input() function allows you to get text input from the user. It displays a prompt to the user and waits for them to type something and press Enter. The function then returns the text that the user entered as a string.

```
name = input("Enter your name: ")
print(f"Hello, {name}!")
```

Important Note: The input() function *always* returns a string, even if the user enters a number. You'll need to convert the input to the appropriate data type if you want to use it as a number.

Handling Numerical Input: Type Conversion is Key

If you want to get numerical input from the user, you'll need to use the int() or float() function to convert the input string to a number.

```
age_str = input("Enter your age: ")
age = int(age_str)   # Convert the input string to an integer
print(f"You are {age} years old.")

#Error checking
if age > 0:
    print ("Valid")
else:
    print ("Invalid age")
```

However, you need to be careful when converting input to numbers. If the user enters something that's not a valid number, the int() or float() function will raise a ValueError. You can handle this using try-except blocks (which we'll cover in more detail later).

A More Robust Approach: Input Validation

It's always a good idea to validate user input to ensure that it's in the correct format and within the expected range. This can help prevent errors and make your programs more robust.

Here's an example of input validation for age:

```python
    while True:
    age_str = input("Enter your age: ")
    try:
        age = int(age_str)
        if age > 0 and age < 150: #Realistic value check
            break  # Exit the loop if the input is valid
        else:
            print("Invalid age. Please enter a positive
number less than 150.")
    except ValueError:
        print("Invalid input. Please enter a number.")

print(f"You are {age} years old.")
```

This code uses a while loop to repeatedly prompt the user for input until they enter a valid age. It also uses a try-except block to handle potential ValueError exceptions.

A Practical Example: A Simple Command-Line Calculator

Let's combine input and output to create a simple command-line calculator:

```python
    num1_str = input("Enter the first number: ")
num2_str = input("Enter the second number: ")

try:
    num1 = float(num1_str)
    num2 = float(num2_str)
    operation = input("Enter the operation (+, -, *, /): ")

    if operation == "+":
        result = num1 + num2
    elif operation == "-":
        result = num1 - num2
    elif operation == "*":
        result = num1 * num2
    elif operation == "/":
        if num2 == 0:
            print("Error: Cannot divide by zero.")
            result = None
        else:
            result = num1 / num2
    else:
        print("Invalid operation.")
        result = None
```

```
    if result is not None:
        print(f"Result: {num1} {operation} {num2} =
{result}")

except ValueError:
    print("Invalid input. Please enter numbers only.")
```

This example demonstrates how to get input from the user, convert it to numbers, perform calculations, and display the results. It also includes error handling to prevent the program from crashing if the user enters invalid input.

In Summary: Connecting Your Program to the User

Input and output are essential for creating interactive and useful programs. By mastering the print() and input() functions, and by implementing robust input validation, you can build programs that seamlessly interact with the user and provide valuable results.

2.5: Comments and Code Style: Speaking the Language of Developers

We've covered how to make the *computer* understand your code. Now, let's talk about how to make *other humans* (including your future self!) understand your code. This is where comments and code style come in.

It's tempting to think of comments and code style as optional extras, as something you can worry about later. But trust me, neglecting them is a recipe for disaster. Writing clean, well-documented code is not just about making it look pretty; it's about making it understandable, maintainable, and collaborative. It's about speaking the language of developers.

Think of it like this: you're writing a book, not just for yourself, but for others to read and learn from. You want to make it as clear and accessible as possible.

Comments: Explaining the "Why," Not Just the "What"

Comments are notes that you add to your code to explain what it does. They are ignored by the Python interpreter but are invaluable for anyone reading your code.

The key is to write comments that explain the *why* behind your code, not just the *what*. Don't just repeat what the code is already doing; explain the reasoning behind it, the purpose it serves, or any assumptions it makes.

Here are some examples of good comments:

```
        # Calculate the area of the rectangle using the
formula: area = length * width
area = length * width

# The following code retrieves the user's profile from the
database.
# It assumes that the user is logged in.
user_profile = get_user_profile(user_id)

# This function implements a binary search algorithm.
# It requires the input list to be sorted.
def binary_search(list, target):
    . . .
```

Notice how these comments explain the purpose or context of the code, not just what it's doing.

Here are some examples of bad comments:

```
    x = 10   # Assign 10 to x (redundant)

x = x + 1   # Increment x (obvious)

#This is a function (duh!)
def my_function():
    . . .
```

These comments are either redundant or obvious, and they don't add any value to the code.

Docstrings: Documenting Your Functions and Classes

Docstrings are special comments that are used to document functions, classes, and modules. They are enclosed in triple quotes ("""Docstring goes here""") and are placed at the beginning of the function, class, or module.

Docstrings serve as the official documentation for your code. They are used by tools like help() and IDEs to display information about your code.

Here's an example of a docstring:

```
def calculate_area(length, width):
"""
Calculates the area of a rectangle.

Args:
    length: The length of the rectangle (in meters).
    width: The width of the rectangle (in meters).

Returns:
    The area of the rectangle (in square meters).
"""
return length * width
```

This docstring explains what the function does, what arguments it takes, and what it returns.

Code Style: Writing Code That's Easy on the Eyes

Code style refers to the way your code is formatted and organized. Consistent code style makes your code easier to read, understand, and maintain.

Python has an official style guide called PEP 8 (Python Enhancement Proposal 8). PEP 8 provides guidelines for things like indentation, line length, variable names, and more.

Following PEP 8 is not mandatory, but it's highly recommended. It makes your code more consistent with the rest of the Python community, and it makes it easier for others to read and understand your code.

PEP 8: Key Guidelines

Here are some of the most important PEP 8 guidelines:

- **Indentation:** Use 4 spaces for indentation. Never use tabs.

```
def my_function():
if True:
    print("Hello")  # Indented 4 spaces
```

- **Line Length:** Keep lines of code less than 79 characters long.

```
    # Break long lines into multiple lines using
parentheses or backslashes.
long_variable_name = (
    "This is a very long string that needs to be broken "
    "into multiple lines."
)
```

- **Blank Lines:** Use blank lines to separate logical sections of code.

```
def my_function():
    # Code to do something

    # Code to do something else

    return result
```

- **Variable Names:** Use descriptive variable names that follow the snake_case convention (lowercase words separated by underscores).

```
user_name = "Alice"
number_of_items = 10
```

- **Comments:** Write clear and concise comments that explain the purpose or context of the code.

Linters: Your Style Enforcement Assistants

Linters are tools that automatically check your code for style violations and other potential problems. They can help you enforce PEP 8 and other coding standards, making your code more consistent and readable.

One popular linter for Python is flake8. You can install it using pip:

```
pip install flake8
```

Then, you can run it on your Python files:

```
flake8 my_file.py
```

The linter will report any style violations or other issues it finds in your code.

Why Bother with All This? The Long-Term Benefits

You might be thinking, "This all seems like a lot of work! Why should I bother with comments and code style?"

Here's why:

- **Readability:** Well-commented and well-styled code is much easier to read and understand. This saves you time and effort when you need to debug or modify your code later.
- **Maintainability:** Readable code is easier to maintain. You'll be able to make changes to your code more easily and with less risk of introducing errors.
- **Collaboration:** If you're working on a team, consistent code style is essential for collaboration. It ensures that everyone is writing code that's easy for everyone else to understand.
- **Professionalism:** Writing clean, well-documented code shows that you take pride in your work and that you care about the quality of your code.

In Summary: Code is Communication

Remember, code is communication. It's not just about telling the computer what to do; it's also about communicating your intentions to other developers (including your future self). By writing clean, well-documented code, you're making your code more valuable and easier to maintain, collaborate on, and reuse.

Chapter 3: Controlling Program Flow: Giving Your Code the Power to Decide and Repeat

Welcome to Chapter 3! In the previous chapter, we learned how to store and manipulate data. Now, we're going to learn how to control the *flow* of your program. This means giving your code the ability to make decisions (using conditional statements) and to repeat actions (using loops). Mastering these concepts will allow you to write programs that are much more dynamic and powerful.

Think of it as adding a steering wheel and an engine to your data. Now, you can actually *go somewhere* with it.

3.1: Conditional Statements: The Crossroads of Your Code

We've learned how to store data and perform operations on it. Now, let's explore how to make your programs *think* – how to make them respond differently based on different situations. This is where conditional statements come in.

Think of conditional statements as the crossroads of your code. They allow your program to choose different paths based on certain conditions, making it more flexible and adaptable. Without them, your programs would always execute the same sequence of instructions, regardless of the input or the circumstances.

The Power of "What If?"

Conditional statements are all about asking "what if?" What if the user enters a valid age? What if the file exists? What if the number is positive? Based on the answers to these questions, your program can execute different code blocks.

The if Statement: The Foundation of Decision-Making

The if statement is the most fundamental conditional statement in Python. It allows you to execute a block of code only if a certain condition is true.

The syntax of the if statement is straightforward:

```
    if condition:
    # Code to execute if the condition is true
```

The condition is an expression that evaluates to either True or False. This expression can be as simple as a single variable or as complex as a combination of variables, operators, and function calls.

Important Note: The code inside the if block *must* be indented. Indentation is how Python determines which statements belong to the if block. Consistent indentation is crucial for writing correct Python code (as we discussed in the section on code style).

Example:

```
    temperature = 25

if temperature > 20:
    print("It's a warm day!")
```

In this example, the condition temperature > 20 is evaluated to True because temperature is 25. Therefore, the code inside the if block is executed, and the message "It's a warm day!" is printed to the console.

If we changed temperature to be, say, 10, the condition would be False and nothing would print.

The else Statement: Providing an Alternative Path

The else statement provides an alternative block of code to execute if the if condition is False. It's like saying, "If this is true, do this; otherwise, do that."

```
    temperature = 15

if temperature > 20:
    print("It's a warm day!")
else:
    print("It's a cool day.")
```

In this example, the condition temperature > 20 is evaluated to False because temperature is 15. Therefore, the code inside the else block is executed, and the message "It's a cool day." is printed to the console.

The elif Statement: Handling Multiple Possibilities

The elif statement (short for "else if") allows you to check multiple conditions in a sequence. It's like saying, "If this is true, do this; otherwise, if this other thing is true, do that; otherwise, do something else."

```
grade = 75

if grade >= 90:
    print("Grade: A")
elif grade >= 80:
    print("Grade: B")
elif grade >= 70:
    print("Grade: C")
elif grade >= 60:
    print("Grade: D")
else:
    print("Grade: F")
```

The elif conditions are evaluated in order. If a condition is True, the corresponding block of code is executed, and the rest of the conditions are skipped. If none of the conditions are True, the code inside the else block (if present) is executed.

Important Note: You can have multiple elif statements, but you can have only one if statement and at most one else statement. The else statement is optional.

Nesting Conditional Statements: Building Complex Decision Trees

You can nest if, elif, and else statements inside each other to create more complex decision trees. This allows you to handle a wide range of scenarios and create highly flexible programs.

```
age = 25
has_license = True

if age >= 16:
    if has_license:
        print("You are eligible to drive.")
    else:
        print("You are old enough to drive, but you don't have a license.")
else:
    print("You are not old enough to drive.")
```

In this example, the outer if statement checks if the person is old enough to drive. If they are, the inner if statement checks if they have a license. This allows you to handle all possible combinations of age and license status.

Truthiness and Falsiness: Python's Hidden Logic

In Python, certain values are considered "truthy" and others are considered "falsy." This means that you can use these values directly in conditional statements without explicitly comparing them to True or False.

Here are some common truthy and falsy values:

- **Truthy:**
  - Any non-zero number
  - Any non-empty string
  - Any non-empty list, tuple, or dictionary
- **Falsy:**
  - 0
  - 0.0
  - "" (empty string)
  - [] (empty list)
  - () (empty tuple)
  - {} (empty dictionary)
  - None

Example:

```
my_list = [1, 2, 3]

if my_list:
    print("The list is not empty.")
else:
    print("The list is empty.")
```

In this example, the condition my_list is evaluated to True because the list is not empty.

This is a handy feature, but it can also be a source of bugs if you're not careful. Make sure you understand which values are considered truthy and falsy in Python.

A Practical Example: A Simple Game

Let's put conditional statements to use in a simple game:

```
import random

secret_number = random.randint(1, 10)
guess = int(input("Guess a number between 1 and 10: "))

if guess == secret_number:
    print("Congratulations! You guessed the number.")
elif guess < secret_number:
    print("Too low! Try again.")
else:
    print("Too high! Try again.")
```

This code generates a random number between 1 and 10 and prompts the user to guess the number. It then uses conditional statements to check if the guess is correct, too low, or too high, and provides appropriate feedback to the user.

In Summary: Conditional Statements are Essential for Creating Intelligent Programs

Conditional statements are a fundamental part of programming. They allow your programs to make decisions, respond to different inputs, and adapt to changing circumstances. By mastering conditional statements, you'll be able to create much more powerful and flexible programs.

3.2: for Loops: Unleashing the Power of Iteration

We've learned how to make decisions with conditional statements. Now, let's explore how to automate repetitive tasks with loops. Loops allow you to execute a block of code multiple times, saving you time and effort.

The for loop is particularly useful for iterating over a sequence of items, such as a list, a string, or a range of numbers. It's like having a robot that can perform the same action on each item in a collection, one after another.

Think of it like this: you have a basket of apples, and you want to wash each apple. You could wash each apple individually, one by one. But it would be much more efficient to use a for loop to automate the process.

The Syntax of the for Loop: A Clear and Concise Structure

The for loop in Python has a clean and elegant syntax:

```
for item in sequence:
    # Code to execute for each item in the sequence
```

- item: This is a variable that will take on the value of each item in the sequence in turn. You can choose any valid variable name for item.
- sequence: This is any iterable object, such as a list, a string, a tuple, a range of numbers, or a dictionary.
- The code inside the loop (the indented block) is executed once for each item in the sequence.

Let's see some examples:

Iterating Over a List: Processing Each Item in Turn

```
fruits = ["apple", "banana", "cherry"]

for fruit in fruits:
    print(f"I love {fruit}!")
```

This code will print the following output:

```
I love apple!
I love banana!
I love cherry!
```

takes on the value of the next fruit in the list, and the code inside the loop is executed.

Iterating Over a String: Accessing Each Character

```
message = "Hello"

for char in message:
    print(char)
```

This code will print each character in the string "Hello" to the console:

```
    H
e
l
l
o
```

In this example, the for loop iterates over the message string. In each iteration, the char variable takes on the value of the next character in the string, and the code inside the loop is executed.

The range() Function: Generating Sequences of Numbers

The range() function is often used with for loops to generate a sequence of numbers. It's particularly useful when you want to repeat a block of code a specific number of times.

range() can take one, two, or three arguments:

- range(stop): Generates a sequence of numbers from 0 up to (but not including) stop.
- range(start, stop): Generates a sequence of numbers from start up to (but not including) stop.
- range(start, stop, step): Generates a sequence of numbers from start up to (but not including) stop, incrementing by step.

Examples:

```python
for i in range(5):
    print(i)   # Output: 0 1 2 3 4

for i in range(1, 6):
    print(i)   # Output: 1 2 3 4 5

for i in range(0, 10, 2):
    print(i)   # Output: 0 2 4 6 8
```

Iterating with Indices: Accessing Elements by Position

Sometimes you need to access the elements of a list by their index (position). You can use the enumerate() function to iterate over a list and get both the index and the value of each element.

```python
fruits = ["apple", "banana", "cherry"]
```

```
for index, fruit in enumerate(fruits):
    print(f"Fruit at index {index}: {fruit}")
```

This code will print the following output:

```
Fruit at index 0: apple
Fruit at index 1: banana
Fruit at index 2: cherry
```

The enumerate() function returns a sequence of tuples, where each tuple contains the index and the value of an element in the list.

A Practical Example: Calculating the Sum of a List of Numbers

Let's put for loops to use in a practical example: calculating the sum of a list of numbers.

```
numbers = [1, 2, 3, 4, 5]
sum = 0

for number in numbers:
    sum += number  # Add the current number to the sum

print(f"The sum of the numbers is: {sum}")  # Output: The sum
of the numbers is: 15
```

This code iterates over the numbers list, adding each number to the sum variable. After the loop has finished, the sum variable contains the total sum of the numbers in the list.

A More Advanced Example: Processing Data from a File

Let's combine for loops with what we learned about string manipulation to process data from a file. Imagine you have a file named "data.txt" with the following content:

```
Name,Age,City
Alice,30,New York
Bob,25,London
Charlie,40,Paris
```

You can use a for loop to read the file line by line and process the data:

```
try:
    with open("data.txt", "r") as file:
        for line in file:
            fields = line.strip().split(",")
            name, age, city = fields
            print(f"Name: {name}, Age: {age}, City: {city}")
except FileNotFoundError:
    print("File not found.")
```

This code opens the "data.txt" file in read mode ("r") and iterates over each line in the file. For each line, it removes any leading or trailing whitespace using strip(), splits the line into fields using , as the delimiter, and then prints the data. Also, a try-except block handles the case where the file doesn't exist.

In Summary: for Loops are Your Automation Powerhouse

for loops are a fundamental part of programming. They allow you to automate repetitive tasks, process data from sequences, and create dynamic and efficient programs. By mastering for loops, you'll gain a powerful tool for tackling a wide range of programming challenges.

3.3: while Loops: The Power of Persistence

We've explored the for loop, which is excellent for iterating over a known sequence of items. Now, let's introduce the while loop, which is perfect for repeating a block of code *until* a certain condition is met. It's like having a robot that keeps performing a task until you tell it to stop.

The while loop is all about persistence. It keeps going and going until the condition you specify becomes false. This makes it incredibly powerful for situations where you don't know in advance how many times you need to repeat the code.

Think of it like this: you're trying to open a locked door. You keep trying different keys until you find the right one. You don't know how many keys you'll have to try, but you keep going until the door opens.

The Syntax of the while Loop: A Simple Yet Powerful Structure

The while loop in Python has a straightforward syntax:

```
while condition:
# Code to execute as long as the condition is true
```

- condition: This is an expression that evaluates to either True or False. As long as the condition is True, the code inside the loop (the indented block) is executed.
- The code inside the loop *must* eventually make the condition False, or the loop will run forever (an infinite loop).

Let's see some examples:

Counting with a while Loop: Repeating Until a Limit is Reached

```
count = 0
while count < 5:
    print(count)
    count += 1  # Increment count to avoid an infinite loop
```

This code will print the numbers 0 to 4 to the console.

In this example, the while loop continues as long as the count variable is less than 5. Inside the loop, we print the value of count and then increment it by 1. This ensures that the condition eventually becomes False, and the loop terminates.

Getting User Input with a while Loop: Repeating Until Valid Input is Provided

```
while True:
    age_str = input("Enter your age: ")
    try:
        age = int(age_str)
        if age > 0 and age < 120:  # Realistic age check
            break  # Exit the loop if the input is valid
        else:
            print("Invalid age. Please enter a positive
number less than 120.")
    except ValueError:
        print("Invalid input. Please enter a number.")

print(f"You are {age} years old.")
```

This code repeatedly prompts the user to enter their age until they enter a valid age (a positive number less than 120). It uses a while True loop, which runs forever unless a break statement is encountered. The try-except block handles potential ValueError exceptions if the user enters something that's not a number.

Simulating a Game Loop: Repeating Until the Game is Over

```python
import random

secret_number = random.randint(1, 10)
guesses_left = 3

while guesses_left > 0:
    guess = int(input(f"Guess a number between 1 and 10 (you
have {guesses_left} guesses left): "))

    if guess == secret_number:
        print("Congratulations! You guessed the number.")
        break  # Exit the loop if the guess is correct
    elif guess < secret_number:
        print("Too low!")
    else:
        print("Too high!")

    guesses_left -= 1  # Decrement guesses_left

if guesses_left == 0:
    print(f"You ran out of guesses. The number was
{secret_number}.")
```

This code simulates a simple guessing game. The user has 3 attempts to guess a secret number. The while loop continues as long as the user has guesses left. If the user guesses the correct number, the loop is terminated using the break statement. If the user runs out of guesses, the loop terminates, and the game is over.

The Peril of Infinite Loops: A Common Pitfall to Avoid

One of the most common mistakes when using while loops is creating an infinite loop. This happens when the condition never becomes False, and the loop runs forever.

Example of an infinite loop:

```
    count = 0

while count < 5:
    print(count)
    #count += 1 #Oops! forgot to increment count
    print("This will print forever!")
```

In this example, the count variable is never incremented, so the condition count < 5 will always be True, and the loop will run forever.

Important Note: If you accidentally create an infinite loop, you can usually stop it by pressing Ctrl+C in the terminal.

Choosing Between for and while Loops: Knowing When to Use Each Tool

So, when should you use a for loop and when should you use a while loop?

- Use a for loop when you know in advance how many times you need to repeat the code (e.g., iterating over a list or a string).
- Use a while loop when you need to repeat the code until a certain condition is met, and you don't know in advance how many times the loop will run.

In other words, use a for loop when you're iterating over a collection, and use a while loop when you're waiting for something to happen.

In Summary: while Loops are Your Gatekeepers

while loops are a powerful tool for creating persistent and flexible programs. They allow you to repeat a block of code until a certain condition is met, making them ideal for situations where you don't know in advance how many times you need to repeat the code. Just be careful to avoid infinite loops!

3.4: break and continue: Fine-Grained Control Over Your Loops

We've learned how to create loops that repeat a block of code multiple times. Now, let's explore how to fine-tune the execution of those loops using the break and continue statements. These statements give you precise control over how your loops behave, allowing you to skip iterations or exit the loop entirely based on specific conditions.

Think of break and continue as emergency exits and detours within your loop. They allow you to deviate from the normal flow of execution when needed.

break: The Emergency Exit

The break statement is used to exit a loop prematurely. When the break statement is encountered, the loop terminates immediately, and the program continues with the next statement after the loop. It's like hitting the emergency stop button on a machine.

The syntax is simple:

```
break
```

Example:

```
numbers = [1, 2, 3, 4, 5]

for number in numbers:
    if number == 3:
        break  # Exit the loop when number is 3
    print(number)

print("Loop finished") #Output outside the loop
```

Output:

```
1
2
Loop finished
```

In this example, the loop iterates through the numbers list. When the number variable is equal to 3, the break statement is executed, causing the loop to terminate immediately. The code after the loop (print("Loop finished")) still runs.

When to Use break:

- **When you've found what you're looking for:** If you're searching for a specific item in a list, you can use break to exit the loop as soon as you find it.
- **When an error occurs:** If an error occurs inside the loop, you can use break to exit the loop and prevent further damage.
- **To implement a "quit" or "exit" command:** In interactive programs, you can use break to allow the user to exit the program.

continue: The Detour

The continue statement is used to skip the current iteration of a loop and continue with the next iteration. When the continue statement is encountered, the rest of the code in the current iteration is skipped, and the loop continues with the next item in the sequence (or the next iteration of the while loop). It's like taking a detour around a construction zone.

The syntax is equally simple:

```
continue
```

Example:

```
numbers = [1, 2, 3, 4, 5]

for number in numbers:
    if number == 3:
        continue  # Skip the iteration when number is 3
    print(number)

print("Loop finished") #output outside the loop
```

Output:

```
1
2
```

```
4
5
Loop finished
```

In this example, the loop iterates through the numbers list. When the number variable is equal to 3, the continue statement is executed, causing the rest of the code in that iteration to be skipped. The loop then continues with the next number in the list. Note that the loop still continues to the end of the list.

When to Use continue:

- **To skip invalid or unwanted data:** If you're processing a list of data and you encounter an invalid or unwanted item, you can use continue to skip that item and continue with the next one.
- **To avoid unnecessary calculations:** If you can determine early in the loop that a particular iteration is not needed, you can use continue to skip the rest of the code in that iteration and save processing time.
- **To handle exceptional cases:** If you encounter an exceptional case that you don't want to handle in the main loop body, you can use continue to skip it and handle it separately later.

A Practical Example: Filtering a List of Numbers

Let's combine break and continue with conditional statements to filter a list of numbers:

```
numbers = [1, 2, -3, 4, -5, 6]

for number in numbers:
    if number < 0:
        continue  # Skip negative numbers
    if number > 5:
        break # Stop at numbers greater than 5

    print(number)   # Output: 1 2 4
```

This code iterates through the numbers list. It skips negative numbers using continue and stops at numbers greater than 5 with break.

A Word of Caution: Use Sparingly

While break and continue can be useful tools, they should be used sparingly. Overuse of these statements can make your code harder to read and understand. It's often better to structure your loops in a way that avoids the need for break and continue, if possible.

Think carefully about whether you really need to use these statements before you add them to your code.

In Summary: break and continue Provide Precise Loop Control

break and continue are powerful tools for fine-tuning the execution of your loops. They allow you to exit the loop prematurely or skip iterations based on specific conditions. However, they should be used with caution, as overuse can make your code harder to read and understand.

3.5: Common Looping Patterns: Elevating Your Loop Game

We've covered the basics of for and while loops, and break and continue. Now, let's move beyond the fundamentals and explore some common looping *patterns* that you'll encounter again and again in your Python programming journey. These patterns are like recipes that you can adapt and reuse to solve a variety of problems.

Mastering these patterns will not only make you a more efficient programmer, but it will also help you think more strategically about how to use loops to achieve your goals.

Pattern 1: Iterating with Indices: Knowing Where You Are in the Sequence

Sometimes, you need to know the index (position) of the item you're currently processing in a loop. This is often the case when you need to modify the list in place, access related elements, or perform calculations based on the index.

While you *could* manually maintain a counter variable, the enumerate() function provides a more elegant and Pythonic way to iterate with indices:

```
my_list = ['a', 'b', 'c']
```

```
for index, value in enumerate(my_list):
    print(f"Index: {index}, Value: {value}")
```

Output:

```
    Index: 0, Value: a
Index: 1, Value: b
Index: 2, Value: c
```

enumerate() returns a sequence of tuples, where each tuple contains the index and the value of an element in the list. This allows you to access both the index and the value in a single loop iteration.

Practical Application: Modifying a List In Place

```
    temperatures = [20, 25, 18, 22, 28]

for index, temp in enumerate(temperatures):
    # Convert Celsius to Fahrenheit
    temperatures[index] = (temp * 9/5) + 32

print(temperatures) #output is in Fahrenheit
```

Pattern 2: Looping Until a Valid Input is Received: Input Validation Loops

We touched on this in the while loop section, but it's worth emphasizing as a common pattern. It's crucial to ensure that the data you're working with is valid, and input validation loops are a common way to achieve this.

```
    while True:
    age_str = input("Enter your age: ")
    try:
        age = int(age_str)
        if 0 < age < 120: #Realistic Age Check
            break  # Valid input, exit loop
        else:
            print("Invalid age. Please enter a positive
number less than 120.")
    except ValueError:
        print("Invalid input. Please enter a number.")

print(f"You are {age} years old.")
```

This pattern combines a while True loop with a try-except block to repeatedly prompt the user for input until they enter a valid age.

Pattern 3: Processing Data from a File, Line by Line: File Processing Loops

File processing is a common task in many Python applications. The most common way to process a file is to read it line by line using a for loop:

```
    try:
    with open("my_data.txt", "r") as file:
        for line in file:
            # Process the line (e.g., split it into fields,
extract data)
            data = line.strip().split(",")
            print(data)
except FileNotFoundError:
    print("File not found!")
```

This pattern opens the file in read mode ("r") and iterates over each line in the file. The strip() method removes any leading or trailing whitespace from the line, and the split(",") method splits the line into fields based on the comma delimiter.

Practical Application: Analyzing Log Files

This pattern is particularly useful for analyzing log files, where each line represents a log entry. You can use string manipulation techniques to extract relevant information from each log entry and perform analysis or reporting.

Pattern 4: Using zip() to Iterate Over Multiple Sequences Simultaneously:

Often, you'll need to iterate over multiple sequences in parallel. The zip() function allows you to combine multiple sequences into a single sequence of tuples, where each tuple contains the corresponding elements from the input sequences.

```
    names = ["Alice", "Bob", "Charlie"]
ages = [30, 25, 40]
cities = ["New York", "London", "Paris"]

for name, age, city in zip(names, ages, cities):
    print(f"{name} is {age} years old and lives in {city}.")
```

This code will print the following output:

```
       Alice is 30 years old and lives in New York.
Bob is 25 years old and lives in London.
Charlie is 40 years old and lives in Paris.
```

Important Note: If the input sequences have different lengths, zip() will stop iterating when the shortest sequence is exhausted.

Pattern 5: Creating a Menu-Driven Program with a while Loop:

Interactive command-line programs often present a menu of options to the user, and then perform actions based on the user's selection. This is typically implemented using a while loop that continues until the user chooses to exit the program.

```python
    while True:
    print("\nMenu:")
    print("1. Option 1")
    print("2. Option 2")
    print("3. Exit")

    choice = input("Enter your choice: ")

    if choice == "1":
        print("Performing action for Option 1...")
        # Code to perform action 1 goes here
    elif choice == "2":
        print("Performing action for Option 2...")
        # Code to perform action 2 goes here
    elif choice == "3":
        print("Exiting program...")
        break  # Exit the loop
    else:
        print("Invalid choice. Please try again.")
```

This pattern provides a basic framework for creating interactive command-line programs.

In Summary: Patterns as Building Blocks

These looping patterns are like building blocks that you can use to construct more complex and sophisticated programs. By mastering these patterns, you'll be well-equipped to tackle a wide range of programming challenges. As you gain more experience, you'll discover even more looping patterns and techniques that will further enhance your programming skills.

Chapter 4: Functions: Building Reusable Code: Your Code's Organizational Superpower

Welcome to Chapter 4! We've learned how to store data, perform operations on it, and control the flow of your program. Now, let's explore how to organize your code into reusable blocks called functions.

Functions are one of the most important concepts in programming. They allow you to break down complex problems into smaller, more manageable pieces. They also allow you to reuse code, which saves you time and effort.

Think of functions as mini-programs within your program. They take some input, perform some calculations, and return some output. They're like the building blocks of your code, and you can combine them in various ways to create complex applications.

4.1: Functions: The Art of Abstraction and Code Reusability

We've reached a point in our Python journey where we need to start thinking about how to organize our code in a more structured way. That's where functions come in. Functions are named blocks of code that perform a specific task. They're like mini-programs within your program, and they're essential for creating well-organized, maintainable, and reusable code.

Think of functions as the tools in your toolbox. Each tool has a specific purpose, and you can use them to build complex structures. Functions allow you to break down a large, complex problem into smaller, more manageable pieces, each of which can be solved independently.

Why Functions Matter: The Core Principles

- **Abstraction:** Functions allow you to abstract away the details of a specific task. You don't need to know *how* the function works internally; you just need to know *what* it does. This simplifies your code and makes it easier to understand.
- **Reusability:** Functions allow you to reuse code multiple times without having to rewrite it. This saves you time and effort, and it also reduces the risk of errors.

- **Modularity:** Functions promote modularity, which means that your code is organized into self-contained modules that can be easily combined and reused. This makes your code easier to maintain and extend.
- **Readability:** Well-named functions make your code more readable and easier to understand. By giving your functions descriptive names, you can communicate the purpose of each block of code to other developers (including your future self).

Defining Functions: The def Keyword and the Code Block

In Python, you define a function using the def keyword, followed by the function name, a list of arguments (optional), and a colon:

```
def function_name(arguments):
# Code to execute
return value #optional
```

Let's break down each part:

- **def:** This keyword signals the start of a function definition.
- **function_name:** This is the name of your function. It should be descriptive and follow the snake_case convention (lowercase words separated by underscores).
- **arguments:** These are the inputs to your function. They are optional. If your function doesn't take any arguments, you still need to include the parentheses ().
- **: (Colon):** The colon indicates the end of the function header.
- **# Code to execute:** This is the code that will be executed when the function is called. It must be indented. The indentation is crucial; Python uses indentation to determine which statements belong to the function.
- **return value:** This is an optional statement that specifies the value that the function returns. If you don't include a return statement, the function will implicitly return None.

A Simple Example: The greet() Function

Let's start with a simple example: a function that greets the user by name:

```
def greet(name):
    """Greets the user by name."""
```

```
print(f"Hello, {name}!")
```

This function takes one argument, name, which represents the name of the user. It then prints a greeting message to the console.

Calling Functions: Bringing Your Code to Life

To execute a function, you need to call it. You do this by using the function name followed by parentheses, passing in any required arguments:

```
greet("Alice") # Output: Hello, Alice!
greet("Bob")   # Output: Hello, Bob!
```

When you call a function, Python executes the code inside the function and then returns to the point where the function was called.

Functions with No Arguments: Performing Tasks Without Inputs

Functions don't always need to take arguments. Sometimes, you just want to define a block of code that performs a specific task without any inputs.

Example:

```
def say_hello():
    """Prints a greeting message."""
    print("Hello!")

say_hello()  # Output: Hello!
```

This function doesn't take any arguments. When you call it, it simply prints a greeting message to the console.

Functions That Return Values: Providing Results to the Caller

Functions can also return values to the caller. This allows you to perform calculations inside the function and then pass the results back to the code that called the function.

To return a value from a function, you use the return statement:

```
def add(x, y):
```

```
"""Returns the sum of x and y."""
return x + y

result = add(5, 3)
print(result) # Output: 8
```

In this example, the add() function takes two arguments, x and y, and returns their sum. The return statement specifies the value that the function returns.

Functions as Building Blocks: Creating Complex Applications

Functions are the building blocks of complex applications. By breaking down a large problem into smaller, more manageable pieces, you can create code that is easier to understand, maintain, and reuse.

As you become more experienced with Python, you'll start to see functions everywhere. You'll use them to encapsulate common tasks, to organize your code into logical modules, and to create reusable components that can be used in multiple applications.

A Practical Example: A Simple Temperature Converter

Let's create a simple program that converts temperatures from Celsius to Fahrenheit:

```
def celsius_to_fahrenheit(celsius):
    """Converts Celsius to Fahrenheit."""
    return (celsius * 9/5) + 32

def get_celsius_from_user():
    """Prompts the user to enter a temperature in Celsius."""
    while True:
        celsius_str = input("Enter a temperature in Celsius: ")
        try:
            celsius = float(celsius_str)
            return celsius
        except ValueError:
            print("Invalid input. Please enter a number.")

celsius = get_celsius_from_user()
fahrenheit = celsius_to_fahrenheit(celsius)
print(f"{celsius} degrees Celsius is equal to {fahrenheit} degrees Fahrenheit.")
```

This example demonstrates how to use functions to break down a complex problem into smaller, more manageable pieces. It also demonstrates how to use function arguments and return values to pass data between functions.

In Summary: Embrace the Power of Functions

Functions are an essential part of Python programming. They allow you to abstract away complexity, reuse code, promote modularity, and improve the readability of your code. By mastering functions, you'll become a much more effective and efficient Python programmer.

4.2: Function Arguments: The Key to Customizing Function Behavior

We've seen how to define and call functions. Now, let's dive deeper into how to pass information *into* functions using arguments. Function arguments are like the ingredients you provide to a chef – they determine the specific dish that the chef will create.

Understanding function arguments is crucial for creating versatile and reusable functions. It allows you to customize the behavior of a function based on the specific inputs you provide.

The Importance of Well-Designed Arguments

The arguments you choose for your functions can significantly impact their usability and readability. Well-designed arguments make your functions easy to use and understand, while poorly designed arguments can lead to confusion and errors.

Think carefully about the arguments your function needs and choose the appropriate types and names for those arguments.

Types of Function Arguments: A Comprehensive Guide

Python supports several types of function arguments, each with its own unique characteristics and use cases. Let's explore them in detail:

1. Positional Arguments: The Foundation

Positional arguments are the most basic type of argument. They are passed to the function in the order they are defined in the function signature.

```python
def describe_pet(name, animal_type):
    """Describes a pet."""
    print(f"I have a {animal_type} named {name}.")

describe_pet("Buddy", "dog") # Output: I have a dog named
Buddy.
```

In this example, name and animal_type are positional arguments. When you call the describe_pet() function, you must provide the arguments in the correct order.

Pitfalls of Positional Arguments:

Positional arguments can become less readable when functions have many arguments. It can be difficult to remember the correct order of the arguments, and it's easy to make mistakes.

2. Keyword Arguments: Clarity and Flexibility

Keyword arguments allow you to pass arguments to a function using their name. This makes your code more readable and less prone to errors, as you don't have to remember the order of the arguments.

```python
def describe_pet(name, animal_type):
    """Describes a pet."""
    print(f"I have a {animal_type} named {name}.")

describe_pet(name="Buddy", animal_type="dog")
describe_pet(animal_type="cat", name="Whiskers") # Order
doesn't matter!
```

With keyword arguments, the order doesn't matter, as long as you specify the name of each argument.

3. Default Arguments: Providing Sensible Defaults

Default arguments allow you to specify a default value for an argument. If the caller doesn't provide a value for that argument, the default value will be used.

```python
def greet(name="World"):
    """Greets the user."""
    print(f"Hello, {name}!")

greet()          # Output: Hello, World! (uses default value)
greet("Alice")   # Output: Hello, Alice!
```

In this example, the name argument has a default value of "World". If you call the greet() function without providing a value for name, the default value will be used.

Important Notes About Default Arguments:

- Default arguments must be defined *after* positional arguments.
- Default arguments are evaluated only once, when the function is defined. This can lead to unexpected behavior if you use mutable objects (like lists or dictionaries) as default arguments.

4. Variable-Length Arguments: Handling an Unknown Number of Inputs

Sometimes, you need to define a function that can accept a variable number of arguments. Python provides two ways to do this:

- *args: This allows you to pass a variable number of *positional* arguments to the function. These arguments are collected into a tuple.
- **kwargs: This allows you to pass a variable number of *keyword* arguments to the function. These arguments are collected into a dictionary.

Let's see some examples:

```python
def print_arguments(*args):
    """Prints all the positional arguments."""
    print(args)

print_arguments(1, 2, 3)  # Output: (1, 2, 3)

def print_keyword_arguments(**kwargs):
    """Prints all the keyword arguments."""
    print(kwargs)
```

```
print_keyword_arguments(name="Alice", age=30, city="New
York") #Output: {'name': 'Alice', 'age': 30, 'city': 'New
York'}
```

These techniques are particularly useful when you need to create functions
that can handle a wide range of inputs.

5. Keyword-Only Arguments: Forcing Clarity

In Python 3, you can use keyword-only arguments to force the caller to use
keyword arguments for certain parameters. This can improve the readability
of your code and prevent accidental errors.

To define keyword-only arguments, you place them after a * in the function
signature:

```
    def calculate_total(price, quantity, *, discount=0.0):
    """Calculates the total price after discount."""
    return (price * quantity) * (1 - discount)

#calculate_total(10, 5, 0.2) #This will cause an error since
discount is keyword only
calculate_total(10, 5, discount=0.2) #This is correct.
```

The discount argument is a keyword-only argument. This means that you
must pass it using its name when you call the function.

Argument Unpacking: Passing Data Structures as Arguments

You can also unpack data structures (like lists and dictionaries) into function
arguments using the * and ** operators:

```
    def add(x, y):
    return x + y

numbers = [5, 3]
result = add(*numbers)   # Unpack the list into positional
arguments
print(result) #Output: 8

def describe_person(name, age, city):
    print(f"Name: {name}, Age: {age}, City: {city}")

person = {"name": "Alice", "age": 30, "city": "New York"}
```

```
describe_person(**person) #unpack dictionary, Output: Name:
Alice, Age: 30, City: New York
```

This technique can be useful when you have a function that expects multiple arguments, and you want to pass them from a data structure.

Best Practices for Designing Function Arguments

- **Use descriptive names:** Choose argument names that clearly communicate the purpose of each argument.
- **Use keyword arguments for complex functions:** This improves readability and reduces the risk of errors.
- **Provide sensible default values:** This makes your functions more flexible and easier to use.
- **Use type hints (as discussed in a previous chapter) to indicate the expected data types:** This helps catch type errors early.
- **Document your arguments:** Use docstrings to explain the purpose of each argument.
- **Consider using keyword-only arguments to enforce clarity.**

In Summary: Mastering Function Arguments for Flexible Code

Function arguments are a powerful tool for customizing the behavior of your functions. By understanding the different types of arguments and how to use them effectively, you can create functions that are versatile, reusable, and easy to understand.

4.3: Return Values: The Output of Your Functional Inventions

We've learned how to pass information *into* functions using arguments. Now, let's explore how to get information *out* of functions using return values. Return values are the results that a function calculates or produces, and they're essential for creating functions that can be used as building blocks in larger programs.

Think of return values as the finished products of your functional inventions. They're the output that you get after providing the function with its inputs.

The Importance of Well-Designed Return Values

The return values you choose for your functions can significantly impact their usability and predictability. Well-designed return values make your functions easy to use and integrate into other code, while poorly designed return values can lead to confusion and errors.

Here's what you should keep in mind:

- **Clarity:** The return value should clearly represent the result of the function's operation.
- **Consistency:** The return value should be consistent across different inputs.
- **Informative:** The return value should provide enough information for the caller to use it effectively.
- **Type Consistency:** It is ideal to return the same datatype throughout all invocations of the function, although Python can handle the return of different data types.

The return Statement: Delivering the Result

In Python, you use the return statement to specify the value that a function returns:

```python
def add(x, y):
    """Returns the sum of x and y."""
    return x + y

result = add(5, 3)
print(result) # Output: 8
```

When the return statement is executed, the function terminates immediately, and the specified value is returned to the caller.

What Happens If You Don't Return Anything? The Implicit None

If a function doesn't have a return statement, it implicitly returns None. None is a special value in Python that represents the absence of a value.

```python
def greet(name):
    """Greets the user (but doesn't return anything)."""
    print(f"Hello, {name}!")

result = greet("Alice")
print(result) # Output: None
```

Although greet successfully prints to the console, it doesn't return any value, so result gets assigned to None.

Important: Be aware of functions that implicitly return None. If you're expecting a function to return a value but it doesn't, you might encounter unexpected behavior in your code.

Returning Multiple Values: The Power of Tuples

Python allows you to return multiple values from a function by packing them into a tuple:

```python
def get_name_and_age():
    """Returns the name and age of a person."""
    name = "Alice"
    age = 30
    return name, age

name, age = get_name_and_age()
print(f"Name: {name}, Age: {age}") # Output: Name: Alice, Age: 30
```

When you return multiple values, Python creates a tuple containing those values. You can then unpack the tuple into separate variables, as shown in the example.

This technique is useful when you want to return several related pieces of information from a function.

Returning Different Data Types: Flexibility with Responsibility

Python is dynamically typed, so you *can* return different data types from a function depending on the input or the circumstances. However, this can make your code harder to understand and maintain.

It's generally best to strive for consistency in your return types. If a function is supposed to return a number, it should always return a number, even if it encounters an error. In such cases, you might consider returning None or raising an exception (which we'll cover later).

Returning Error Codes: A Traditional Approach (But Not Always the Best)

In some languages, it's common to use return values to indicate whether a function succeeded or failed. For example, a function might return 0 to indicate success and a non-zero value to indicate an error.

While this approach is still used in Python, it's generally better to use exceptions to handle errors (which we'll cover in a later chapter). Exceptions provide a more structured and informative way to handle errors, and they can help you write more robust code.

Practical Example: A Function That Performs Multiple Operations

Let's create a function that performs multiple operations on a number and returns the results:

```
def process_number(number):
    """Calculates the square, cube, and square root of a
number."""
    square = number * number
    cube = number * number * number
    square_root = number ** 0.5
    return square, cube, square_root

square, cube, square_root = process_number(4)
print(f"Square: {square}, Cube: {cube}, Square Root:
{square_root}")
```

This function calculates the square, cube, and square root of a number and returns the results as a tuple. This allows you to perform multiple calculations with a single function call.

In Summary: Design Return Values with Intention

Return values are the output of your functional inventions. By designing them carefully and intentionally, you can create functions that are easy to use, predictable, and reliable.

4.4: Variable Scope: Your Variables' Neighborhoods and Boundaries

We've learned how to define and call functions, and how to pass information in and out of them. Now, let's explore a concept that's crucial for avoiding confusion and errors in your code: variable scope. Variable scope refers to the region of your code where a variable is accessible or "visible." It's like defining the neighborhood where a variable "lives."

Understanding variable scope is essential for writing code that behaves predictably and for preventing naming conflicts. Without a clear understanding of scope, you might accidentally modify variables in unexpected places, or you might encounter errors because a variable is not accessible where you think it should be.

Think of variable scope as establishing boundaries and rules for variable access in different parts of your program.

The Different "Neighborhoods": Local, Global, and Enclosing (Briefly)

Python has several types of scope, but the most important ones to understand are:

- **Local Scope:** Variables defined *inside* a function have local scope. They are only accessible within that function. Think of it as a variable that lives only within the walls of the function.

    ```python
    def my_function():
        x = 10  # x is a local variable
        print(f"Inside the function: x = {x}")

    my_function()  # Output: Inside the function: x = 10
    #print(x)  # This would cause an error: NameError: name 'x'
    is not defined
    ```

    Outside of my_function, the variable x simply doesn't exist. Trying to access it will result in a NameError.

- **Global Scope:** Variables defined *outside* of any function have global scope. They are accessible from *anywhere* in your code, including inside functions. Think of it as a variable that's publicly accessible to everyone.

```
x = 10  # x is a global variable

def my_function():
    print(f"Inside the function: x = {x}")

my_function()  # Output: Inside the function: x = 10
print(f"Outside the function: x = {x}")  # Output: Outside
the function: x = 10
```

- **Enclosing Scope (Brief Introduction):** This comes into play when you have nested functions (a function defined inside another function). The inner function can access variables from the outer function's scope. We'll touch on this briefly later.

The LEGB Rule: Python's Scope Search Order

When you try to access a variable, Python searches for it in a specific order, following the LEGB rule:

1. **Local:** The scope of the current function.
2. **Enclosing:** The scope of any enclosing functions.
3. **Global:** The global scope (outside of any functions).
4. **Built-in:** The built-in scope (e.g., functions like print(), len()).

Python searches in this order until it finds the variable. If it doesn't find the variable, it raises a NameError.

Modifying Global Variables Inside Functions: The global Keyword (Use with Caution!)

If you want to modify a global variable *inside* a function, you need to use the global keyword to explicitly declare that you're referring to the global variable:

```
x = 10  # x is a global variable

def my_function():
    global x  # Declare that we're using the global x
    x = 20  # Modify the global x
    print(f"Inside the function: x = {x}")
```

```
my_function() #Output: Inside the function: x = 20
print(f"Outside the function: x = {x}")   # Output: Outside
the function: x = 20
```

Without the global keyword, Python would create a *new* local variable named x inside the function, and the global x would remain unchanged.

Important Warning: While using global might seem convenient, it's generally considered bad practice. Modifying global variables inside functions can make your code harder to understand and debug, and it can lead to unexpected side effects. Favor passing variables as arguments and returning values instead.

Example of a Common Mistake: Unintentional Local Variable

Here's a classic example of a scope-related mistake:

```
    x = 10

def my_function():
    x = x + 5   # Trying to modify the global x
    print(f"Inside the function: x = {x}")

my_function()
```

This code will raise an UnboundLocalError because Python assumes that you're trying to assign a value to a *local* variable x before it has been assigned a value. To fix this, you would need to use the global keyword (but again, it's better to avoid this situation altogether if possible).

A Better Approach: Passing Variables as Arguments and Returning Values

Instead of relying on global variables, the best practice is to pass variables as arguments to your functions and return values:

```
    def my_function(x):
    """Adds 5 to x and returns the result."""
    x = x + 5
    return x

x = 10
x = my_function(x) #now re-assign the result to x
```

```
print(f"Outside the function: x = {x}") #Output: Outside the
function: x = 15
```

This approach makes your code more explicit, easier to understand, and less prone to errors.

Nested Functions and Enclosing Scope (A Brief Glimpse)

In Python, you can define functions inside other functions. The inner function can access variables from the outer function's scope (the enclosing scope).

```
def outer_function():
    x = 10

    def inner_function():
        print(f"Inside the inner function: x = {x}") # can
access x from outer

    inner_function()

outer_function() #Output: Inside the inner function: x = 10
```

This is a powerful feature, but it can also make your code more complex. It's important to understand how scope works when you're working with nested functions.

Practical Example: A Configuration System

While we often discourage direct modification of globals, consider a configuration system as one potential use case, with appropriate caution and design.

```
CONFIG = {'debug': False}

def enable_debug():
    global CONFIG
    CONFIG['debug'] = True

def is_debug_enabled():
    return CONFIG['debug']

print(f"Debug Enabled at Start: {is_debug_enabled()}") #
False
enable_debug()
```

```
print(f"Debug Enabled After Update: {is_debug_enabled()}") #
True
```

In Summary: Master the Art of Scope Management

Understanding variable scope is essential for writing correct and
maintainable Python code. By following the LEGB rule and avoiding the use
of global variables (whenever possible), you can create code that is more
predictable, easier to debug, and less prone to errors.

4.5: Anonymous Functions: The Art of the One-Liner

We've learned how to define and call regular functions using the def
keyword. Now, let's explore a more concise way to create functions: lambda
expressions. Lambda expressions, also known as anonymous functions, are
small, unnamed functions that can be defined in a single line of code.

Think of lambda expressions as quick, disposable functions that you can
create on the fly. They're particularly useful for simple operations that don't
require a full-fledged function definition.

The Syntax of the lambda Expression: A Compact Form

The syntax of a lambda expression is as follows:

```
lambda arguments: expression
```

- **lambda:** This keyword indicates that you're creating an anonymous
  function.
- arguments: These are the inputs to the function. They are optional.
- : (Colon): The colon separates the arguments from the expression.
- expression: This is the code that the function executes. It *must* be a
  single expression.

A Simple Example: Squaring a Number

Let's start with a simple example: a lambda expression that squares a
number:

```
square = lambda x: x * x
```

```
result = square(5)
print(result) # Output: 25
```

In this example, we create a lambda expression that takes one argument, x, and returns its square. We assign the lambda expression to the variable square. Now, we can call the lambda expression just like a regular function.

Important: Lambda expressions are limited to a single expression. You can't include multiple statements or complex control flow logic inside a lambda expression.

When to Use lambda Expressions: A Guide to Appropriate Use

Lambda expressions are most useful in the following situations:

- **For simple, one-line operations:** If you need to perform a simple calculation or transformation, a lambda expression can be more concise than a regular function definition.
- **When you need a function for a short period of time:** If you only need a function for a single use, a lambda expression can be a convenient way to create it without cluttering your code with a full function definition.
- **With higher-order functions:** Lambda expressions are often used as arguments to higher-order functions like map(), filter(), and sort(). These functions take other functions as arguments, and lambda expressions provide a concise way to define those functions inline.

Common Use Case: Sorting with a Custom Key

A classic use case is providing a custom comparison key to the sort() method or the sorted() function. For example, let's say you have a list of tuples and you want to sort it based on the second element of each tuple:

```
data = [(1, 5), (2, 3), (3, 1)]

data.sort(key=lambda item: item[1]) #Sort by the second
element in the tuple
print(data) #Output: [(3, 1), (2, 3), (1, 5)]
```

Without a lambda expression, you would need to define a separate function to extract the second element of each tuple. The lambda expression provides a concise way to do this inline.

Higher-Order Functions: map() and filter()

Lambda expressions are often used with higher-order functions like map() and filter().

- map(function, iterable): Applies a function to each item in an iterable and returns a new iterable with the results.
- filter(function, iterable): Filters an iterable based on a function that returns True for items to keep and False for items to discard.

Examples:

```
numbers = [1, 2, 3, 4, 5]
# Square each number in the list using map() and a lambda
expression
squared_numbers = list(map(lambda x: x * x, numbers))
print(squared_numbers)  # Output: [1, 4, 9, 16, 25]

# Filter out even numbers using filter() and a lambda
expression
odd_numbers = list(filter(lambda x: x % 2 != 0, numbers))
print(odd_numbers)  # Output: [1, 3, 5]
```

In these examples, the lambda expressions provide a concise way to define the functions that are used by map() and filter().

When to Avoid lambda Expressions: Readability Considerations

While lambda expressions can be useful for concise code, they can also make your code harder to read if they become too complex.

Here are some situations where you should avoid lambda expressions:

- **When the expression is too long or complex:** If the expression inside the lambda expression is too long or complex, it can make the code difficult to read. In these cases, it's better to use a regular function definition.

- **When you need to reuse the function multiple times:** If you need to use the function in multiple places, it's better to define it as a regular function so that you can give it a descriptive name and easily reuse it.
- **When you need to add documentation:** Lambda expressions don't support docstrings, so you can't add documentation to explain what they do. If you need to document your function, you should use a regular function definition.

Key principle: Code is read far more than it is written. Optimize for readability, and if a named function makes your code clearer, then use it instead of a lambda.

Practical Example: A Function That Takes a Function as an Argument

Let's create a function that takes another function as an argument and applies it to a list of numbers:

```
def apply_function(numbers, func):
    """Applies a function to each number in a list."""
    results = []
    for number in numbers:
        results.append(func(number))
    return results

numbers = [1, 2, 3, 4, 5]

# Apply the square function using a lambda expression
squared_numbers = apply_function(numbers, lambda x: x * x)
print(squared_numbers) # Output: [1, 4, 9, 16, 25]

#Apply a function defined by def:
def cube (x):
    return x*x*x
cubed_numbers = apply_function(numbers, cube)
print(cubed_numbers) #Output: [1, 8, 27, 64, 125]
```

In Summary: Lambda Expressions - Use with Intention

Lambda expressions are a powerful tool for creating concise code, but they should be used with caution. Use them for simple operations that don't require a full-fledged function definition, and avoid them when readability is a concern.

Chapter 5: Working with Data Structures: Organizing Your Data for Success

Welcome to Chapter 5! We've learned how to store data using variables and how to write functions to process that data. Now, let's explore how to organize your data using data structures.

Data structures are specialized containers that allow you to store and manage collections of data in an organized and efficient way. Choosing the right data structure for a particular task can significantly improve the performance and readability of your code.

Think of data structures as the different types of organizers you might use in your office: folders for documents, drawers for supplies, and shelves for books. Each organizer has its own strengths and weaknesses, and you choose the one that's best suited for the task at hand.

5.1: Lists: The Ever-Present, Incredibly Useful Python Container

Lists are one of Python's most essential and ubiquitous data structures. You'll find yourself using them constantly, in almost every project you undertake. They're versatile, flexible, and relatively easy to use, making them an ideal starting point for understanding data structures. But don't let their simplicity fool you; lists are also powerful tools for building complex applications.

Think of lists as dynamic, adaptable containers that can hold a collection of items in a specific order. It is the first tool in any Python developer's toolbox.

Understanding Lists: Order, Mutability, and Dynamic Typing

To truly understand lists, you need to grasp three key concepts:

- **Order:** Lists maintain the order in which elements are added. This is important for many applications, such as storing a sequence of events, processing data in a specific order, or representing a deck of cards.
- **Mutability:** Lists are mutable, which means you can change their contents after they are created. You can add, remove, or modify

elements in a list as needed. This makes lists ideal for situations where the data is dynamic and changing.

- **Dynamic Typing:** Lists can contain elements of any data type, and you can even mix different data types in the same list. While technically possible, it's generally good practice to keep your lists homogeneous (containing elements of the same type) for better code readability and maintainability.

These characteristics make lists a flexible and powerful tool for managing collections of data.

Creating Lists: From Simple to Sophisticated

There are several ways to create lists in Python, each with its own use cases:

- **Literal Notation ([]): The Most Common Approach**

  This is the most straightforward and commonly used way to create a list. Simply enclose the elements in square brackets, separated by commas:

  ```python
  my_list = [1, 2, 3, "hello", True]
  ```

- **The list() Constructor: Conversion Power**

  The list() constructor can be used to create a list from other iterable objects, such as strings, tuples, sets, or even generators. This is useful for converting data from one format to another.

  ```python
  my_string = "Python"
  my_list = list(my_string)   # Output: ['P', 'y', 't', 'h', 'o', 'n']

  my_tuple = (1, 2, 3)
  my_list = list(my_tuple)    # Output: [1, 2, 3]
  ```

- **Empty Lists: Starting from Scratch**

  Creating an empty list is useful when you want to add elements to the list later, either manually or programmatically:

```
    my_list = []
#my_list.append(item) # Add code here
```

Accessing List Elements: The Power of Indexing

You can access individual elements in a list using their index (position).
Remember that list indices start at 0.

```
    my_list = [10, 20, 30, 40, 50]

print(my_list[0])  # Output: 10 (first element)
print(my_list[2])  # Output: 30 (third element)
print(my_list[-1]) # Output: 50 (last element, negative
indexing)
```

Key Insights:

- **Positive Indexing:** Starts from the beginning of the list, with index 0 representing the first element.
- **Negative Indexing:** Starts from the end of the list, with index -1 representing the last element. This is a convenient way to access elements from the end of the list without knowing its length.
- **IndexError:** Trying to access an index that is out of range will raise an IndexError. Be careful to avoid this error by checking the length of the list before accessing elements.

Modifying Lists: A Dynamic Dance

Lists are mutable, meaning you can change their contents after they are created. Python offers a variety of methods for modifying lists:

- **Element Assignment:** Changing the value of an existing element at a specific index:

```
    my_list = [10, 20, 30]
my_list[1] = 25  # Change the second element to 25
print(my_list) # Output: [10, 25, 30]
```

- **append(): Adding to the End**

Adds an element to the end of the list. This is a common way to dynamically build a list as you process data.

```
my_list = [10, 20, 30]
my_list.append(40)
print(my_list) # Output: [10, 20, 30, 40]
```

- **insert(): Precise Placement**

Inserts an element at a specific index, shifting the existing elements to make room. This is useful when you need to maintain a specific order in the list.

```
my_list = [10, 20, 30]
my_list.insert(1, 15) # Insert 15 at index 1
print(my_list) # Output: [10, 15, 20, 30]
```

- **remove(): Targeted Removal**

Removes the *first* occurrence of a specific value from the list.

```
my_list = [10, 20, 30, 20]
my_list.remove(20) # Removes the first occurrence of 20
print(my_list) # Output: [10, 30, 20]
```

- **pop(): Removal and Retrieval**

Removes the element at a specific index *and returns it*. This is useful when you need to both remove an element from the list and get its value.

```
my_list = [10, 20, 30]
removed_element = my_list.pop(1) # Remove element at index 1
print(my_list)            # Output: [10, 30]
print(removed_element)   # Output: 20
```

Slicing Lists: Creating Subsets with Ease

Slicing allows you to create a new list containing a subset of the elements from an existing list. This is a powerful tool for extracting specific portions of data.

```
my_list = [10, 20, 30, 40, 50]

print(my_list[1:4])    # Output: [20, 30, 40] (elements from
index 1 up to, but not including, index 4)
print(my_list[:3])     # Output: [10, 20, 30] (from the
beginning up to, but not including, index 3)
print(my_list[3:])     # Output: [40, 50] (from index 3 to the
end)
print(my_list[::2])    # Output: [10, 30, 50] (every other
element)
print(my_list[::-1])   # Output: [50, 40, 30, 20, 10]
(reversed list)
```

List Methods: A Treasure Trove of Functionality

Lists come equipped with a rich set of built-in methods for performing common operations. Some of the most useful include:

- **len():** Returns the number of elements in the list.
- **append():** Adds an element to the end of the list.
- **insert():** Inserts an element at a specific index.
- **remove():** Removes the first occurrence of a specific value.
- **pop():** Removes the element at a specific index and returns it.
- **index():** Returns the index of the first occurrence of a specific value.
- **count():** Returns the number of times a specific value appears in the list.
- **sort():** Sorts the list in place (modifies the original list). Use the key argument for custom sorting.
- **reverse():** Reverses the list in place (modifies the original list).
- **copy():** Returns a shallow copy of the list (creates a new list with the same elements).

Understanding List References vs. Copies: A Crucial Distinction

When you assign one list to another using the = operator, you're not creating a new list; you're creating a *reference* to the original list. This means that if you modify the original list, the changes will also be reflected in the new list.

```
list1 = [1, 2, 3]
list2 = list1 # list 2 is a pointer that refers to list 1

list1.append(4)
print(list2) # Output: [1, 2, 3, 4]
```

If you want to create a *new* list with the same elements, you need to use the copy() method or slicing:

```
    list1 = [1, 2, 3]
list2 = list1.copy()   # Create a shallow copy
#or list2 = list1[:] #alternative way to copy

list1.append(4)
print(list2) # Output: [1, 2, 3] - list2 is unchanged
```

Understanding the difference between references and copies is essential for avoiding unexpected behavior in your code.

List Methods: A Rich Toolkit

Lists provide a rich set of methods for performing common operations. Here are some of the most useful:

- **len():** Returns the length of the list (number of elements).
- **append():** Adds an element to the end of the list.
- **insert():** Inserts an element at a specific index.
- **remove():** Removes the first occurrence of a specific value.
- **pop():** Removes the element at a specific index and returns it.
- **index():** Returns the index of the first occurrence of a specific value.
- **count():** Returns the number of times a specific value appears in the list.
- **sort():** Sorts the list in place (modifies the original list).
- **reverse():** Reverses the list in place (modifies the original list).
- **copy():** Returns a shallow copy of the list (creates a new list with the same elements).

In Summary: Lists - Simple, Powerful, and Ever-Present

Lists are a fundamental data structure in Python. By mastering their characteristics, methods, and nuances, you'll be well-equipped to tackle a wide range of programming challenges. Always remember to choose the right data structure for the job, and use the power of lists to organize and manipulate your data effectively.

5.2: List Comprehensions: Python's Elegant List Builder

We've explored the power and versatility of lists, but Python offers an even more elegant way to create them: list comprehensions. List comprehensions provide a concise and readable syntax for creating new lists based on existing iterables. They are a cornerstone of Pythonic code and a must-have tool for any serious Python programmer.

Think of list comprehensions as a way to express the creation of a list in a single, declarative statement. Instead of writing a multi-line loop, you can create a new list with a single, expressive line of code.

The Anatomy of a List Comprehension: A Clear and Concise Structure

The syntax of a list comprehension is as follows:

```
new_list = [expression for item in iterable if condition]
```

Let's break down each part:

- **expression:** This is the value that will be added to the new list. It can be any valid Python expression, including calculations, function calls, or conditional expressions.
- **for item in iterable:** This is the same as a for loop, where item is a variable that takes on the value of each element in the iterable.
- **if condition (optional):** This is a conditional expression that filters the elements from the iterable. Only elements that satisfy the condition will be included in the new list.

The entire list comprehension is enclosed in square brackets [], indicating that it creates a new list.

From Loops to Comprehensions: A Transformation

Let's see how a traditional for loop can be transformed into a list comprehension:

- **Traditional Loop:**

```
numbers = [1, 2, 3, 4, 5]
```

```
squared_numbers = []

for number in numbers:
    squared_numbers.append(number * number)

print(squared_numbers)  # Output: [1, 4, 9, 16, 25]
```

- **List Comprehension:**

```
numbers = [1, 2, 3, 4, 5]
squared_numbers = [number * number for number in numbers]

print(squared_numbers)  # Output: [1, 4, 9, 16, 25]
```

As you can see, the list comprehension achieves the same result as the traditional loop, but in a more concise and readable way.

Adding Conditions: Filtering Your Data

You can use the optional if condition to filter the elements from the iterable:

- **Traditional Loop:**

```
numbers = [1, 2, 3, 4, 5]
even_numbers = []

for number in numbers:
    if number % 2 == 0:
        even_numbers.append(number)

print(even_numbers)  # Output: [2, 4]
```

- **List Comprehension:**

```
numbers = [1, 2, 3, 4, 5]
even_numbers = [number for number in numbers if number % 2 ==
0]

print(even_numbers)  # Output: [2, 4]
```

The if number % 2 == 0 condition filters the elements, only including even numbers in the new list.

Beyond Simple Values: Transformations and Calculations

The expression in a list comprehension can be any valid Python expression, allowing you to perform complex transformations and calculations on the elements:

```python
words = ["hello", "world", "python"]

uppercase_words = [word.upper() for word in words] # Make
them uppercase
print(uppercase_words) #Output: ['HELLO', 'WORLD', 'PYTHON']

word_lengths = [len(word) for word in words] # Get their
lengths
print (word_lengths) #Output: [5, 5, 6]
```

When to Use List Comprehensions: A Matter of Style and Readability

List comprehensions are a powerful tool, but they're not always the best choice.

- **Use list comprehensions for simple transformations and filtering.** If the logic is complex or requires multiple lines of code, it's better to use a traditional loop.
- **Prioritize readability.** If a list comprehension makes your code harder to understand, it's better to use a traditional loop.
- **Consider the length of the code.** If a list comprehension becomes too long, it can be difficult to read. In these cases, it's better to break it up into smaller parts or use a traditional loop.

Remember: Code is read far more often than it is written. Strive for clarity and readability above all else.

A Practical Example: Processing Data from a File (Again!)

Let's revisit our file processing example from Chapter 6 and use a list comprehension to extract the names from a list of lines:

```python
try:
    with open("names.txt", "r") as file:
        names = [line.strip() for line in file] #Remove
leading whitespace from each line and set each line as an
element in the names file.
    print(names)
```

```
except FileNotFoundError:
    print ("The file does not exist")
```

This elegant one-liner achieves the same result as a multi-line loop, demonstrating the power and conciseness of list comprehensions.

In Summary: Master List Comprehensions for Pythonic Code

List comprehensions are a cornerstone of Pythonic code, providing a concise, readable, and efficient way to create new lists based on existing iterables. By mastering list comprehensions, you'll be able to write more elegant, expressive, and maintainable code.

5.3: Dictionaries: Mapping Your Way to Efficient Data Retrieval

We've explored lists, ordered collections where elements are accessed by their position (index). Now, let's introduce a different kind of collection: the dictionary. Dictionaries are unordered collections of key-value pairs, where each key is associated with a specific value.

Think of a dictionary as a real-world dictionary. You look up a word (the key) to find its definition (the value). Dictionaries in Python provide a similar mechanism for storing and retrieving data based on meaningful keys. They also go by names such as 'associative arrays' and 'hashmaps' in other languages.

The Power of Key-Value Pairs: Modeling Relationships

The key-value pair structure makes dictionaries incredibly useful for modeling real-world relationships. For example:

- **User Profiles:** You can use a dictionary to store information about a user, with the keys representing attributes like "name", "age", "email", and the values representing the corresponding data.
- **Configuration Settings:** You can use a dictionary to store configuration settings for your application, with the keys representing the setting names and the values representing the setting values.

- **Inventory Management:** You can use a dictionary to store inventory data, with the keys representing product IDs and the values representing the quantity in stock.

The ability to associate data with meaningful keys is what makes dictionaries so powerful and versatile.

Creating Dictionaries: A Few Different Approaches

Python offers several ways to create dictionaries:

- **Curly Braces {}: The Most Common Notation**

  The most common way to create a dictionary is to use curly braces {} and specify the key-value pairs:

  ```
  my_dict = {"name": "Alice", "age": 30, "city": "New York"}
  ```

- **The dict() Constructor: From Iterables to Dictionaries**

  The dict() constructor can be used to create a dictionary from an iterable of key-value pairs (e.g., a list of tuples):

  ```
  my_list = [("name", "Alice"), ("age", 30), ("city", "New York")]
  my_dict = dict(my_list)   # Create a dictionary from the list of tuples
  ```

- **Dictionary Comprehensions: Concise Creation**

  Similar to list comprehensions, dictionary comprehensions provide a concise way to create dictionaries based on existing iterables.

  ```
  numbers = [1, 2, 3, 4, 5]
  squared_dict = {number: number * number for number in numbers}
  #Output: {1: 1, 2: 4, 3: 9, 4: 16, 5: 25}
  ```

Accessing Dictionary Values: The Art of the Lookup

You can access the value associated with a key using square brackets []:

```
    my_dict = {"name": "Alice", "age": 30, "city": "New
York"}

print(my_dict["name"])   # Output: Alice
print(my_dict["age"])    # Output: 30
```

However, if you try to access a key that doesn't exist in the dictionary, you'll get a KeyError. To avoid this, you can use the get() method:

```
    print(my_dict.get("name"))        # Output: Alice
print(my_dict.get("occupation"))  # Output: None (no error)
print(my_dict.get("occupation", "Unknown"))  # Output:
Unknown (default value)
```

The get() method returns the value associated with the key if it exists, or a default value (if specified) if the key doesn't exist.

Modifying Dictionaries: A Dynamic Data Store

Dictionaries are mutable, so you can add, change, and delete entries after they are created:

- **Adding a New Entry:**

```
    my_dict["occupation"] = "Software Engineer" #add the
occupation and value
```

- **Changing an Existing Entry:**

```
    my_dict["age"] = 31 #modify a value for the same key
```

- **Deleting an Entry:**

```
    del my_dict["city"] #delete the city entry
```

Dictionary Methods: Essential Tools for Working with Dictionaries

Dictionaries provide several methods for performing common operations:

- **len():** Returns the number of key-value pairs in the dictionary.
- **keys():** Returns a view object containing the keys in the dictionary.
- **values():** Returns a view object containing the values in the dictionary.
- **items():** Returns a view object containing the key-value pairs in the dictionary as tuples.
- **get():** Returns the value associated with a key, or a default value if the key doesn't exist.
- **pop():** Removes the key-value pair associated with a key and returns the value.
- **popitem():** Removes and returns an arbitrary key-value pair from the dictionary (useful for emptying a dictionary).
- **copy():** Returns a shallow copy of the dictionary.
- **update():** Updates the dictionary with the key-value pairs from another dictionary or iterable object.

Key-Value Views: Dynamic Reflections

The keys(), values(), and items() methods return *view objects*, not static lists. This means that the view objects are dynamically updated whenever the dictionary changes.

```
my_dict = {"name": "Alice", "age": 30}

keys = my_dict.keys()
print(keys)  # Output: dict_keys(['name', 'age'])

my_dict["city"] = "New York" #Add to dict

print(keys)  # Output: dict_keys(['name', 'age', 'city']) -
The view is updated!
```

This behavior can be useful when you need to keep track of the keys, values, or items in a dictionary as it changes.

Dictionaries vs. Lists: Choosing the Right Tool

When should you use a dictionary and when should you use a list?

- **Use a list when:**
  - You need to store an ordered collection of items.
  - You need to access elements by their position (index).
  - The order of the elements is important.

95

- **Use a dictionary when:**
  - You need to store a collection of key-value pairs.
  - You need to access values based on meaningful keys.
  - The order of the elements is not important.

Practical Example: A Simple Phonebook

Let's create a simple phonebook using a dictionary:

```
    phonebook = {
  "Alice": "123-456-7890",
  "Bob": "987-654-3210",
  "Charlie": "555-123-4567"
}

name = input("Enter a name: ")

if name in phonebook:
    print(f"The phone number for {name} is
{phonebook[name]}.")
else:
    print(f"Sorry, no number is listed for {name}")
```

In Summary: Dictionaries - Where Data Finds Its Meaning

Dictionaries are a powerful and versatile data structure that allow you to store and retrieve data based on meaningful keys. By mastering dictionaries, you'll be able to create code that is more efficient, readable, and expressive.

5.4: Tuples: The Reliable, Unchanging Sequences

We've explored lists, the dynamic and adaptable workhorses of Python data structures. Now, let's introduce a more rigid, yet equally valuable, counterpart: the tuple. Tuples are ordered collections of items, much like lists, but with one crucial difference: they are *immutable*. This means that once a tuple is created, you cannot change its contents. You can't add, remove, or modify elements in a tuple.

At first glance, this immutability might seem like a limitation. But in reality, it's a source of strength, enabling tuples to play a unique and important role in Python programming.

Think of tuples as representing fixed, unchanging collections of data, like the coordinates of a city, the RGB values of a color, or the dimensions of a rectangle.

Why Immutability Matters: Data Integrity and Performance

Immutability is the defining characteristic of tuples, and it has several important implications:

- **Data Integrity:** Immutability ensures that the data stored in a tuple cannot be accidentally modified. This is crucial when you need to guarantee the consistency and reliability of your data.
- **Hashability:** Because tuples are immutable, they are *hashable*. This means that they can be used as keys in dictionaries and as elements in sets. Lists, being mutable, cannot be used in these ways.
- **Performance:** Tuples are generally faster than lists, especially for read-only operations. Python can optimize tuple storage and access because it knows that the contents will not change.
- **Safety:** Because tuples are immutable, they are inherently thread-safe, meaning they can be safely accessed and shared between multiple threads without the risk of data corruption.

Creating Tuples: A Few Simple Ways

Creating tuples is similar to creating lists, but with a few key differences:

- **Parentheses (): The Standard Notation**

  The most common way to create a tuple is to enclose the elements in parentheses (), separated by commas:

  ```
  my_tuple = (1, 2, 3, "hello", True)
  ```

- **Implicit Tuples: Commas are Key**

  You can also create tuples without parentheses, as long as there are at least two items separated by commas:

  ```
  my_tuple = 1, 2, 3
  ```

However, it's generally good practice to use parentheses for clarity.

- **The Single-Element Tuple: A Trailing Comma**

  To create a tuple with a single item, you *must* include a trailing comma:

  ```
  my_tuple = (1,)
  ```

  Without the trailing comma, Python will interpret (1) as a simple expression, not a tuple.

- **The tuple() Constructor: Conversion Tool**

  Like lists, you can create tuples from other iterables using the tuple() constructor:

  ```
  my_list = [1, 2, 3]
  my_tuple = tuple(my_list) #creating tuple from a list
  ```

Accessing Tuple Elements: Just Like Lists

You can access individual elements in a tuple using their index, just like with lists:

```
my_tuple = (10, 20, 30, 40, 50)

print(my_tuple[0])  # Output: 10
print(my_tuple[-1]) # Output: 50
```

Tuple Operations: What You *Can* Do

While you can't modify the contents of a tuple, you can perform several operations on tuples:

- **Slicing:** Create new tuples containing a subset of the elements from an existing tuple.
- **Concatenation:** Combine two or more tuples to create a new tuple.
- **Iteration:** Iterate over the elements in a tuple using a for loop.

- **Membership Testing:** Check if a value is present in a tuple using the in operator.

Examples:

```
my_tuple = (10, 20, 30, 40, 50)

print(my_tuple[1:4])    # Output: (20, 30, 40) (slicing)

new_tuple = my_tuple + (60, 70) # Output (10, 20, 30, 40, 50,
60, 70) - (Concatenation)
```

Tuple Unpacking: Assigning Values with Elegance

Tuple unpacking is a powerful feature that allows you to assign the values in a tuple to multiple variables in a single line of code:

```
coordinates = (10, 20) #make object

x, y = coordinates #assign each of the coordinates to each
new object in this line

print(f"X: {x}, Y: {y}") #print each value
```

This technique is often used to return multiple values from a function or to iterate over a list of tuples.

When to Use Tuples: A Matter of Choice

When should you use a tuple and when should you use a list?

- **Use a tuple when:**
  - You need to store a collection of items that should not be modified.
  - You need to use the collection as a key in a dictionary or as an element in a set (because tuples are hashable).
  - You want to ensure data integrity and prevent accidental modification.
  - You want to optimize performance for read-only operations.
- **Use a list when:**
  - You need to store a collection of items that might need to be modified.

- You need to add, remove, or change elements in the collection.
- The order of the elements is important.

Practical Example: Representing RGB Colors

Tuples are often used to represent RGB colors, as the red, green, and blue values are typically fixed:

```
red = (255, 0, 0)
green = (0, 255, 0)
blue = (0, 0, 255)

print(f"Red: {red}")  #show the numbers
```

In Summary: Tuples - Reliability in the Face of Change

Tuples are a valuable data structure in Python, providing a way to store immutable sequences of data. By understanding their characteristics, methods, and use cases, you'll be able to choose the right tool for the job and write more efficient and reliable code.

5.5: Sets: The Power of Uniqueness and Mathematical Operations

We've explored lists and tuples, ordered collections that can contain duplicate values. Now, let's introduce a different kind of collection: the set. Sets are unordered collections of *unique* items. This means that a set can only contain one copy of each value.

Think of sets as mathematical sets. They're useful for representing collections where membership is the primary concern, and the order of the elements is not important. They allow you to perform efficient set operations like union, intersection, and difference, making them ideal for tasks like filtering data, finding common elements, and identifying unique items.

The Beauty of Uniqueness: Eliminating Redundancy

The defining characteristic of sets is their ability to store only unique values. If you try to add a duplicate value to a set, it will simply be ignored.

This makes sets incredibly useful for removing duplicates from a list or other iterable object:

```
my_list = [1, 2, 2, 3, 3, 3, 4, 4, 4, 4]
unique_numbers = set(my_list) #remove repeat numbers

print(unique_numbers)  # Output: {1, 2, 3, 4}
```

Notice that the set() constructor automatically removes the duplicate values from the list, leaving only the unique elements.

Creating Sets: A Couple of Options

You can create sets in Python using curly braces {} or the set() constructor:

- **Curly Braces {}: Direct and Concise**

   The most common way to create a set is to enclose the elements in curly braces {}, separated by commas:

   ```
   my_set = {1, 2, 3, 4, 5}
   ```

- **The set() Constructor: From Other Iterables**

   You can also create sets from other iterables, such as lists, tuples, or strings, using the set() constructor:

   ```
   my_list = [1, 2, 3, 4, 5]
   my_set = set(my_list) #creating tuple from list

   my_string = "hello"
   my_set = set(my_string) #create set from string

   print (my_set)
   ```

Important Note: To create an *empty* set, you *must* use the set() constructor. Using {} will create an empty *dictionary*, not an empty set.

Set Operations: Unleashing the Power of Mathematics

Sets provide several methods for performing common set operations:

- ### union() or | (Union): Combining Sets

  Returns a new set containing all the elements in both sets.

  ```
          set1 = {1, 2, 3, 4, 5}
  set2 = {3, 4, 5, 6, 7}

  print(set1.union(set2))   # Output: {1, 2, 3, 4, 5, 6, 7}
  print(set1 | set2)        # Output: {1, 2, 3, 4, 5, 6, 7}
  (shorthand)
  ```

- ### intersection() or & (Intersection): Finding Common Elements

  Returns a new set containing only the elements that are in both sets.

  ```
          set1 = {1, 2, 3, 4, 5}
  set2 = {3, 4, 5, 6, 7}

  print(set1.intersection(set2))   # Output: {3, 4, 5}
  print(set1 & set2)               # Output: {3, 4, 5}
  (shorthand)
  ```

- ### difference() or - (Difference): Finding Unique Elements

  Returns a new set containing only the elements that are in the first set but not in the second set.

  ```
          set1 = {1, 2, 3, 4, 5}
  set2 = {3, 4, 5, 6, 7}

  print(set1.difference(set2))   # Output: {1, 2}
  print(set1 - set2)             # Output: {1, 2}
  (shorthand)
  ```

- ### symmetric_difference() or ^ (Symmetric Difference): Finding Exclusively Unique Elements

  Returns a new set containing only the elements that are in either set, but not in both.

  ```
          set1 = {1, 2, 3, 4, 5}
  set2 = {3, 4, 5, 6, 7}
  ```

```
print(set1.symmetric_difference(set2)) # Output: {1, 2, 6, 7}
print(set1 ^ set2)                      # Output: {1, 2, 6, 7}
(shorthand)
```

These set operations are incredibly efficient, making sets a powerful tool for working with large collections of data.

Membership Testing: A Speed Boost

Checking if an element is present in a set is much faster than checking if an element is present in a list or tuple. This is because sets use a hash table to store their elements, allowing for very fast lookups.

In general, use a list if order is important, and a set if membership testing is common.

When to Use Sets: A Guide to the Right Choice

- **Use a set when:**
    - You need to store a collection of unique items.
    - You need to perform set operations (union, intersection, difference).
    - You need to test for membership frequently.
    - The order of the elements is not important.
- **Avoid sets when:**
    - You need to store duplicate values.
    - You need to access elements by their position (index).
    - The order of the elements is important.

Practical Example: Finding Unique Words in a Text File

Let's combine sets with our file handling skills to find the unique words in a text file:

```
import re

try:
    with open("text.txt", "r", encoding="utf-8") as file:
        text = file.read().lower() #lower case for better comparison
        words = re.findall(r'\b\w+\b', text) #Regular expression to pull words from text.
```

```
        unique_words = set(words) #Convert to set to remove
repeats
    print(f"The file contains {len(unique_words)} unique
words.")
    print (unique_words)
except FileNotFoundError:
    print ("File not found")
```

This code reads the text file, converts it to lowercase (for case-insensitive counting), extracts the words using a regular expression, converts the list of words to a set to remove duplicates, and then prints the number of unique words.

In Summary: Sets: Unlock Data and Mathematical Excellence

Sets are a powerful and efficient data structure for working with collections of unique items. By understanding their characteristics, methods, and use cases, you'll be able to solve a variety of programming problems with elegance and efficiency.

Chapter 6: File Handling Basics: Connecting Your Programs to the Outside World

Welcome to Chapter 6! So far, we've been working with data that's either hardcoded into our programs or entered by the user. Now, let's explore how to read data from files and write data to files, allowing your programs to interact with the outside world.

File handling is a fundamental skill for any programmer. It allows you to persist data, process large datasets, and integrate your programs with other systems. Whether you're reading configuration files, analyzing log data, or creating reports, file handling is an essential tool in your programming arsenal.

Think of file handling as establishing a connection between your program and the storage on your computer. Your program can then read information from files on the hard drive, and write information to create or modify files.

6.1: Reading Data from Files: Opening the Door to External Data

We've reached a crucial step in our Python journey: learning how to read data from files. This is the gateway to bringing information from the external world into your programs. It's no longer just about what you type in or what's already in your code; it's about unlocking the vast amounts of data stored in files.

Reading data from files is fundamental for countless tasks: processing log files, analyzing datasets, importing configuration settings, and much more. It's the foundation for building programs that can interact with the real world.

The open() Function: Your Key to Unlocking Files

The first step in reading data from a file is to open it using the open() function. It's your key to unlocking the file's content.

```
file = open("my_file.txt", "r")   # "r" signifies read mode
```

As we mentioned earlier, the open() function takes two essential arguments:

- **The file path:** This is the location of the file you want to access. It can be a relative path (relative to the location of your Python script) or an absolute path (the full path from the root directory).
- **The file mode:** This specifies the *purpose* of opening the file. In this case, "r" tells Python that we want to open the file for *reading*. We'll explore other file modes in more detail later.

Important Note: The open() function, by itself, *doesn't* actually read any data from the file. It simply establishes a connection between your program and the file, preparing it for reading.

Choosing the Right Reading Method: A Strategic Decision

Once you've opened the file, you have several options for reading its content, each with its own strengths and weaknesses:

- **read(): Grabbing the Whole Enchilada (Use with Caution!)**

  The read() method reads the *entire* content of the file and returns it as a single string.

  ```python
  file = open("my_file.txt", "r")
  content = file.read()
  print(content)
  file.close()
  ```

  This is simple, but it's only suitable for small files that can easily fit into your computer's memory. For large files, read() can consume a significant amount of memory and potentially crash your program.

- **readline(): One Line at a Time**

  The readline() method reads a *single* line from the file, including the newline character (\n) at the end.

  ```python
  file = open("my_file.txt", "r")
  line1 = file.readline()
  line2 = file.readline()
  print(line1)
  print(line2)
  file.close()
  ```

This is useful for processing files line by line, which is more memory-efficient than reading the entire file at once. However, you still need to call readline() multiple times to read the entire file.

- **readlines(): A List of Lines**

  The readlines() method reads *all* the lines from the file and returns them as a *list* of strings.

```
file = open("my_file.txt", "r")
lines = file.readlines()
print(lines)
file.close()
```

  This is more memory-efficient than read(), but it still loads the entire file into memory as a list. It's suitable for moderately sized files where you need to access all the lines at once.

- **Iterating Over the File Object: The Pythonic Way**

  The most Pythonic and memory-efficient way to read a file line by line is to iterate directly over the file object in a for loop:

```
file = open("my_file.txt", "r")
for line in file:
    print(line.strip()) # use .strip() to remove newline characters
file.close()
```

  This approach reads the file line by line without loading the entire file into memory. It's the preferred method for reading large files, as it minimizes memory usage. The .strip() function removes any leading and trailing whitespace (including the newline character) from each line before printing it.

Closing the File: A Crucial Step for Resource Management

After you're finished reading from a file, it's essential to close it using the close() method:

```
file.close()
```

Closing the file releases the resources that were allocated when the file was opened. This is important for several reasons:

- **Preventing Resource Leaks:** If you don't close the file, your program might hold onto the file handle, preventing other programs from accessing the file.
- **Ensuring Data Integrity:** Closing the file ensures that any buffered data is written to disk.
- **Releasing System Resources:** Closing the file releases system resources that are used to manage the file.

Handling Potential Errors: Robust Code for Real-World Scenarios

File operations can sometimes fail due to various reasons:

- The file might not exist.
- You might not have permission to read the file.
- The file might be corrupted.

It's good practice to handle these potential errors using a try-except block:

```
try:
    file = open("my_file.txt", "r")
    for line in file:
        print(line.strip())
    file.close() # ensure file is closed even if loop
encounters errors
except FileNotFoundError:
    print("Error: The file 'my_file.txt' was not found.")
except PermissionError:
    print("Error: You do not have permission to read this
file.")
except Exception as e: #Catch all other exceptions
    print(f"An unexpected error occurred: {e}")
finally:
    # Always close the file, even if an exception occurred
    if 'file' in locals() and hasattr(file, 'close'): #check
if file is defined and has a close method
        file.close()
```

This code attempts to open and read the file. If a FileNotFoundError occurs, the code in the first except block is executed, and an error message is printed.

This example also shows a broader "catch-all" Exception, in case the file exists, but there's a file corruption or other IO issue. Finally, it also checks that the file variable exists and has a close method before calling close() to avoid further errors if the file could not be opened in the first place.

The finally Block: Ensuring Cleanup Even in the Face of Errors

The finally block is executed *no matter what* happens in the try block, even if an exception occurs. This makes it the perfect place to close the file, ensuring that it's always closed properly.

A Practical Example: Reading a Configuration File

Let's say you have a configuration file named "config.txt" with the following content:

```
username=Alice
password=secret
database=my_database
```

You can use file handling to read these settings into your program:

```
config = {} #empty dictionary

try:
    file = open("config.txt", "r")
    for line in file:
        line = line.strip()
        if line: # Ignore blank lines, but also empty lines
after strip
            key, value = line.split("=", 1) #Limit to one
split only in case values also contain "="
            config[key] = value
    file.close()
except FileNotFoundError:
    print("Error: The configuration file 'config.txt' was not
found.")
except ValueError:
    print("Config file corrupted!")
except Exception as e:
    print (f"Other error: {e}")
finally:
    if 'file' in locals() and hasattr(file, 'close'):
        file.close()

print(config)
```

This code opens the "config.txt" file, reads each line, splits it into key-value pairs, and stores them in a dictionary called config. It also handles potential errors such as the file not being found or the file having an invalid format.

In Summary: Respecting Files and Handling Data Carefully

Reading data from files is a powerful way to bring information into your programs, but it's important to do it carefully. Choose the right reading method for the size and structure of your file, always close your files properly, and handle potential errors to prevent your programs from crashing.

6.2: Writing Data to Files: Leaving Your Mark on the Digital World

We've mastered the art of reading data from files, bringing external information into our programs. Now, let's learn how to do the reverse: how to *write* data to files, persisting information and leaving our mark on the digital world.

Writing data to files is essential for saving results, creating reports, generating configuration files, and many other tasks. It's the key to making your programs not just *process* data but also *produce* data that can be used by other programs or analyzed later.

The open() Function Revisited: Preparing for Writing

Just like with reading, the first step in writing data to a file is to open it using the open() function. However, instead of using read mode ("r"), we'll use either write mode ("w") or append mode ("a"), or the less common exclusive creation ("x").

```
file = open("my_file.txt", "w") # "w" for write mode
# or
file = open("my_file.txt", "a") # "a" for append mode
# or
file = open("my_file.txt", "x") # "x" for exclusive creation
mode
```

110

Let's examine the implications of each mode:

- **Write Mode ("w"): A Clean Slate (with a Warning)**

  Write mode ("w") opens the file for writing and *truncates* it, meaning it completely erases any existing content. If the file doesn't exist, it creates a new one.

  Use extreme caution when using write mode, as it can easily lead to data loss if you're not careful. Always double-check that you're writing to the correct file and that you don't need to preserve any existing content.

- **Append Mode ("a"): Adding to the Story**

  Append mode ("a") opens the file for writing, but *preserves* any existing content. All new data will be added to the *end* of the file. If the file doesn't exist, it creates a new one.

  Append mode is ideal when you want to add data to a file without overwriting the existing content, such as when logging events or collecting data over time.

- **Exclusive Creation Mode ("x"): Creating Only When Safe**

  Exclusive Creation ("x") creates a *new* file for writing, but *only* if the file *does not* already exist. If the file exists, the open() call will raise a FileExistsError. This is a good choice when you want to be sure you're not accidentally overwriting an existing file.

The write() Method: Putting Data into the File

Once you've opened the file in the appropriate mode, you can write data to it using the write() method:

```
file = open("my_file.txt", "w")
file.write("This is the first line.\n")
file.write("This is the second line.\n")
file.close()
```

The write() method takes a string as an argument and writes it to the file. It's important to remember to explicitly add newline characters (\n) to separate lines, as write() doesn't automatically add them.

Writing Multiple Lines: A More Concise Approach

If you have a list of lines that you want to write to a file, you can use the writelines() method:

```
lines = ["This is the first line.\n", "This is the
second line.\n"]
file = open("my_file.txt", "w")
file.writelines(lines)
file.close()
```

The Importance of Data Formatting: Making Your Data Readable

When writing data to files, it's crucial to format the data in a way that makes it easy to read and process later. This is especially important when writing structured data, such as CSV files or JSON files.

Consider using appropriate delimiters (e.g., commas, tabs) to separate fields, and use consistent data types and formats.

Character Encoding: Ensuring Your Characters Are Represented Correctly

Character encoding is a system for representing characters (letters, numbers, symbols) as numbers. Different character encodings can represent different sets of characters.

The most common character encoding is UTF-8, which can represent almost all characters from all languages.

When writing data to files, it's important to specify the correct character encoding to ensure that your characters are represented correctly. You can do this by passing the encoding argument to the open() function:

```
file = open("my_file.txt", "w", encoding="utf-8")
file.write("This file contains Unicode characters: こんにちは
\n")
file.close()
```

If you don't specify the encoding, Python will use the default encoding for your system, which might not be UTF-8. This can lead to problems if you're working with files that contain characters outside of the default encoding.

Error Handling: Protecting Your Data

Just like with reading files, it's important to handle potential errors when writing data to files. This can prevent data loss and ensure that your program behaves gracefully in the face of unexpected problems.

```python
try:
    file = open("my_file.txt", "w", encoding="utf-8")
    file.write("This is some data.\n")
    file.close() #close inside try, and also in finally
except PermissionError:
    print("Error: You do not have permission to write to this file.")
except Exception as e:
    print(f"An unexpected error occurred: {e}")
finally: #ensure file is closed
    if 'file' in locals() and hasattr(file, 'close'): #check if file is defined and has a close method
        file.close()
```

Practical Example: Writing a Configuration File

Let's create a program that writes a configuration file:

```python
config = {
    "username": "Alice",
    "password": "secret",
    "database": "my_database"
}

try:
    file = open("config.txt", "w", encoding="utf-8")
    for key, value in config.items():
        file.write(f"{key}={value}\n")
    file.close()
except PermissionError:
    print("Error: You do not have permission to write to the config file.")
except Exception as e:
    print(f"Other Error {e}")
finally:
    if 'file' in locals() and hasattr(file, 'close'):
        file.close()
```

In Summary: Write with Responsibility and Attention to Detail

Writing data to files is a powerful way to persist information from your programs, but it's important to do it responsibly and with attention to detail. Choose the appropriate writing mode, format your data carefully, specify the correct character encoding, and handle potential errors to ensure that your data is written correctly and safely.

6.3: File Modes: Defining the Rules of Engagement

We've seen the open() function used to connect your Python code to files, but to wield it effectively, you need to understand its various 'modes'. File modes are like the rules of engagement. They determine *how* your program is allowed to interact with a file – whether it's for reading, writing, or both, and how existing content should be treated. Choosing the right file mode is crucial for preventing data loss, avoiding errors, and ensuring that your program behaves as intended.

Think of file modes as setting the permissions for your program's access to a file.

The Core Modes: Read, Write, Append, and Exclusive Creation

The foundation of file handling in Python rests on these four core modes:

- **"r" (Read): The Observer**

  "r" opens the file in *read-only* mode. Your program can only read data from the file; it cannot modify it in any way. This is the default mode if you don't specify one.

  If the file doesn't exist, Python will raise a FileNotFoundError.

  When to use: When you only need to read data from a file and you don't want to risk accidentally modifying it. Log file analyzers or data import routines are good candidates.

- **"w" (Write): The Overwriter (Handle with Care!)**

"w" opens the file in *write* mode. If the file exists, its *entire content is deleted* – it's like starting with a completely blank slate. If the file doesn't exist, it creates a new one.

Use with extreme caution! This mode is appropriate only when you explicitly want to replace the existing content of a file with new data.

When to use: When you are creating a new file or completely replacing the contents of an existing file. Generating a report from scratch could fall into this category.

- **"a" (Append): The Historian**

  "a" opens the file in *append* mode. If the file exists, new data is added to the *end* of the file, preserving the existing content. If the file doesn't exist, it creates a new one.

  When to use: When you want to add data to an existing file without overwriting the existing content. Log files, data collection scripts, or adding entries to a database file often use this approach.

- **"x" (Exclusive Creation): The Safety Net**

  "x" opens the file in *exclusive creation* mode. This is like saying, "Create this file, but only if it *doesn't* already exist." If the file exists, Python will raise a FileExistsError.

  When to use: When you want to create a new file and you want to be absolutely sure that you're not accidentally overwriting an existing file. This is particularly useful in situations where data integrity is paramount.

Binary vs. Text Modes: Decoding the Data

In addition to the core modes, you can also specify whether you want to open the file in *text* mode (the default) or *binary* mode.

- **Text Mode ("t"): For Human-Readable Data**

  When you open a file in text mode (e.g., "rt", "wt", "at"), Python assumes that the file contains text data and automatically handles the encoding and decoding of characters. This is the appropriate mode for reading and writing text files, such as configuration files, source code, or CSV files.

- **Binary Mode ("b"): For Raw Data**

  When you open a file in binary mode (e.g., "rb", "wb", "ab"), Python treats the file as a sequence of bytes and doesn't perform any encoding or decoding. This is the appropriate mode for reading and writing non-text files, such as images, audio files, or compressed archives.

  Why is this important? Text mode handles different operating systems' ways of indicating "new line" which are OS specific. Binary mode reads data "as is."

The "+" Mode: The Dual Threat (Use with Caution!)

The "+" mode allows you to open a file for *both* reading and writing. You can combine it with other modes to create more specific combinations:

- "r+": Opens the file for reading and writing. The file pointer is positioned at the beginning of the file.
- "w+": Opens the file for reading and writing. The file is truncated (existing content is deleted).
- "a+": Opens the file for reading and writing. The file pointer is positioned at the end of the file.

Use with care! These modes can be tricky to use correctly, as you need to be careful about the file pointer position and how it affects reading and writing.

Putting It All Together: Examples

Let's see some examples of how to use different file modes:

```python
    # Read a text file
try:
    with open("my_text_file.txt", "r", encoding="utf-8") as
file:
        content = file.read()
        print(content)
except FileNotFoundError:
    print("Text File not found")

# Write to a text file (overwriting existing content)
```

```
try:
    with open("my_text_file.txt", "w", encoding="utf-8") as
file:
        file.write("This is the new content.\n")
except PermissionError:
    print("No permission to write")

# Append to a text file
try:
    with open("my_text_file.txt", "a", encoding="utf-8") as
file:
        file.write("This is an additional line.\n")
except PermissionError:
    print ("no permission to write")

# Read a binary file (e.g., an image)
try:
    with open("my_image.jpg", "rb") as file:
        image_data = file.read()
    #Do something with the image data here
    print(f"The image is {len(image_data)} bytes")
except FileNotFoundError:
    print ("Image file not found")

# Create a new file (only if it doesn't exist)
try:
    with open("new_file.txt", "x", encoding="utf-8") as file:
        file.write("This is the initial content.\n")
except FileExistsError:
    print("Error: The file already exists.")
except Exception as e:
    print (f"Other error: {e}")
```

In Summary: Choosing the Right Mode for the Job

File modes are essential for controlling how your program interacts with files. By understanding the different modes and their implications, you can write code that is safer, more predictable, and more efficient. Always take the time to choose the right mode for the task at hand, and be especially careful when using write mode to avoid accidental data loss.

6.4: The with Statement: Your Safety Net for File Handling

We've learned how to open files, read from them, and write to them. But there's a subtle danger lurking: what happens if something goes wrong while you're working with a file? What if an error occurs before you have a chance to close it?

That's where the with statement comes in. It's your safety net for file handling, ensuring that your files are always closed properly, even if an error occurs. It might seem like a small detail, but it can make a big difference in the reliability and robustness of your code. It's the best practice, and you should default to it every time you work with files.

Think of the with statement as an automatic door closer. It ensures that the door is always closed behind you, even if you trip and fall on your way out.

Why the with Statement Matters: Resource Management and Error Handling

The with statement addresses two key concerns:

- **Resource Management:** When you open a file, your program acquires a limited system resource called a "file handle." If you don't close the file properly, that file handle remains in use, potentially preventing other programs from accessing the file or leading to resource exhaustion.
- **Error Handling:** If an error occurs while you're working with a file (e.g., a FileNotFoundError, a PermissionError, or a ValueError), your code might not reach the file.close() statement. This leaves the file open and potentially corrupts your data.

The with statement solves both of these problems by guaranteeing that the file is always closed, regardless of whether an error occurs.

The Syntax of the with Statement: Clean and Concise

The syntax of the with statement is clean and concise:

```
with open("my_file.txt", "r") as file:
# Code to work with the file
content = file.read()
print(content)
# File is automatically closed here
```

Let's break down each part:

- **with:** This keyword signals the start of a with statement.
- **open("my_file.txt", "r"):** This is the expression that creates the context. In this case, it opens the file "my_file.txt" in read mode.
- **as file:** This assigns the file object returned by open() to the variable file. You can choose any valid variable name for this.
- **The indented block:** This is the code that will be executed within the context. You can perform any operations on the file within this block.
- When the with block is finished (either normally or due to an error), the file is automatically closed.

Key benefit: By using the with statement, you no longer need to explicitly call file.close(). Python takes care of it for you.

A Practical Example: Reading a File with Error Handling and Automatic Cleanup

Let's see how to use the with statement to read a file with robust error handling and automatic cleanup:

```
try:
    with open("my_file.txt", "r", encoding="utf-8") as file:
        content = file.read()
        print(content)
except FileNotFoundError:
    print("Error: The file 'my_file.txt' was not found.")
except Exception as e: #Handle any other error
    print(f"An error occurred: {e}")

# No need for a finally block to close the file! The 'with'
statement does it for us
```

In this example, the with statement ensures that the file is closed properly, even if a FileNotFoundError occurs. You no longer need a finally block to close the file.

Beyond Files: The Power of Context Managers

The with statement isn't just for file handling. It can be used with any object that supports the "context management protocol." These objects are called *context managers*.

A context manager is an object that defines what should happen when entering and exiting a with block. It typically has two methods:

119

- __enter__(): This method is called when the with block is entered. It can perform setup tasks, such as acquiring a resource.
- __exit__(): This method is called when the with block is exited. It can perform cleanup tasks, such as releasing a resource.

File objects, like the ones returned by open(), are context managers. That's why you can use them with the with statement.

Creating Your Own Context Managers (A Glimpse into Advanced Python)

You can create your own context managers using classes and the __enter__() and __exit__() methods. This allows you to manage resources and ensure proper cleanup in your own code. (This is beyond the scope of this introductory book, but is included here for more advanced learners.)

In Summary: Embrace the with Statement for Safe and Reliable File Handling

The with statement is an essential tool for writing robust and reliable file handling code. It ensures that your files are always closed properly, preventing resource leaks and data corruption. By using the with statement, you can simplify your code and focus on the core logic of your program.

6.5: Basic File Processing Techniques: From Raw Data to Meaningful Insights

We've learned the individual tools for file handling: opening, reading, writing, and managing resources with with. Now, let's put it all together and explore some common file processing techniques that will allow you to transform raw data into meaningful insights.

File processing is more than just reading and writing; it's about extracting, transforming, and loading (ETL) data to solve real-world problems. It's about taking raw, unstructured data and turning it into something useful.

Pattern 1: Reading and Processing Data Line by Line

This is the most fundamental and versatile file processing technique. It involves reading a file line by line and performing some operation on each line. We've already seen this pattern in previous sections, but let's formalize it:

```python
    try:
    with open("my_data.txt", "r", encoding="utf-8") as file:
        for line in file:
            line = line.strip()  # Remove leading/trailing
whitespace
            # Process the line (e.g., split it into fields,
extract data)
            print(f"Processing line: {line}")  # Replace with
your logic
except FileNotFoundError:
    print("Error: The file was not found.")
except Exception as e:
    print(f"Other File Processing Error: {e}")
```

Key Elements:

- **Error Handling:** The try-except block ensures that your program handles potential errors gracefully.
- **Line Stripping:** line.strip() removes any leading or trailing whitespace from the line, ensuring that you're working with clean data.
- **Processing Logic:** The print(f"Processing line: {line}") placeholder should be replaced with your specific logic for processing each line of data. This might involve splitting the line into fields, extracting specific values, or performing calculations.

When to Use: This pattern is ideal for processing large files that don't fit into memory. It's also useful when you need to process each line of data independently. Log file analysis, configuration file parsing, and data transformation tasks often employ this approach.

Practical Application: Counting Words in a Text File

Let's use this pattern to count the number of words in a text file:

```python
    word_count = 0

try:
    with open("my_text.txt", "r", encoding="utf-8") as file:
        for line in file:
            line = line.strip()
            words = line.split()  # Split the line into words
```

```
            word_count += len(words)  # Add the number of
words to the count
    print(f"The file contains {word_count} words.")
except FileNotFoundError:
    print("Error: The file was not found.")
except Exception as e:
    print(f"A File Processing error occurred: {e}")
```

Pattern 2: Reading and Writing Structured Data (CSV)

CSV (Comma Separated Values) is a common format for storing tabular data. Python provides the csv module to simplify reading and writing CSV files.

```
    import csv

#Reading a CSV File
try:
  with open("my_data.csv", "r", newline="", encoding="utf-8")
as file:
        reader = csv.reader(file) #Create csv reader object
        header = next(reader) #skip header

        for row in reader:
          #Process each row
          print (row)
except FileNotFoundError:
    print ("CSV File not found")
except Exception as e:
    print (f"File Processing Error: {e}")

#Writing to a CSV file
data = [["Name", "Age", "City"], ["Alice", "30", "NY"],
["Bob", "25", "London"]]

try:
    with open("output.csv", "w", newline="", encoding="utf-
8") as file:
        writer = csv.writer(file)
        writer.writerows(data)
    print ("CSV written successfully")
except PermissionError:
    print("No Permission to write")
except Exception as e:
    print (f"File Writing error: {e}")
```

Key Points:

- **import csv:** Imports the csv module.
- **csv.reader(file):** Creates a CSV reader object that can be used to iterate over the rows in the file.
- **csv.writer(file):** Creates a CSV writer object that can be used to write rows to the file.
- **newline="":** This is important for handling line endings correctly on different operating systems.

When to Use: This pattern is ideal for reading and writing data that is already in CSV format or that can be easily converted to CSV format. It's often used for importing and exporting data from spreadsheets or databases.

Practical Application: Analyzing CSV Data

Let's use this pattern to read a CSV file and calculate the average age of the people in the file:

```python
import csv

total_age = 0
num_people = 0

try:
    with open("people.csv", "r", newline="", encoding="utf-8") as file:
        reader = csv.reader(file)
        header = next(reader) #Skip header, advance to next line

        for row in reader:
            try:
                age = int(row[1])   # Assuming age is in the second column
                total_age += age
                num_people += 1
            except ValueError:
                print(f"Invalid age in row: {row}") #Print a warning if bad data
except FileNotFoundError:
    print ("File not found")
except Exception as e:
    print (f"File Processing Error: {e}")

if num_people > 0:
    average_age = total_age / num_people
    print(f"The average age is: {average_age:.2f}")
else:
```

```
    print("No people found in the file.")
```

Pattern 3: Using Regular Expressions for Advanced Text Processing

Sometimes, you need to extract data from files that don't follow a consistent format. In these cases, regular expressions can be a powerful tool.

```python
    import re

try:
    with open("log.txt", "r", encoding="utf-8") as file:
        for line in file:
            match = re.search(r"ERROR:\s+(.*)", line)  #
Regex to search for error, and retrieve message
            if match:
                error_message = match.group(1) #get the
captured group (the error message)
                print(f"Error message: {error_message}")
except FileNotFoundError:
    print("File not found.")
except Exception as e:
    print (f"File Processing Error: {e}")
```

Key Points:

- **import re:** Imports the re module for regular expressions.
- **re.search(pattern, string):** Searches for a pattern in a string and returns a match object if found.
- **match.group(1):** Returns the first capturing group in the match.

When to Use: This pattern is useful for extracting data from unstructured text files, such as log files or web pages. Regular expressions can be complex, but they provide a powerful way to extract specific information from text.

In Summary: Combining Techniques to Extract Meaning from Files

These file processing techniques are like the ingredients in a recipe. By combining them in different ways, you can create programs that can process a wide variety of file formats and extract meaningful insights from your data. As you gain more experience, you'll develop your own set of preferred techniques and patterns for working with files.

Chapter 7: Modules and Packages: Expanding Your Python Universe

Welcome to Chapter 7! We've learned how to write code and organize it into functions. Now, let's explore how to reuse code written by others (and how to organize your *own* code for reuse) using modules and packages.

Modules and packages are essential for building larger, more complex Python applications. They allow you to break down your code into manageable units and to leverage the vast ecosystem of third-party libraries that are available for Python.

Think of modules and packages as pre-built components that you can plug into your own projects. They save you time and effort by providing ready-made solutions to common problems.

7.1: Importing Modules: Standing on the Shoulders of Giants

We've learned how to create our own functions, and that's great for encapsulating reusable logic within a single program. But what if you want to reuse code *across* multiple programs, or even better, leverage code written by *other* developers? That's where modules come in.

Importing modules is a cornerstone of Python programming. It allows you to tap into a vast library of pre-written code, saving you time, effort, and potential reinvention of the wheel. Think of it as standing on the shoulders of giants – building upon the work of others to reach new heights.

In essence, you are unlocking the functionality that the other developer has created in their file, which saves you a lot of time.

What are Modules, Exactly? A Closer Look

A module is simply a Python file containing Python code: functions, classes, variables, and even executable code. When you import a module, you're essentially loading that file into your current program and making its contents available for use.

Python offers two main kinds of modules:

- **Built-in modules:** These are part of the Python standard library and are always available without requiring installation. They provide essential functionality for common tasks.
- **External modules (packages):** These are third-party libraries that are not included with Python but can be easily installed using pip. They provide a vast range of specialized functionality, from web development to data science.

The import Statement: Your Gateway to Code Reuse

The import statement is the primary way to bring modules into your Python programs:

```python
import math

# Use functions from the math module
result = math.sqrt(16)
print(result)  # Output: 4.0
```

When you use import module_name, Python searches for a file named module_name.py (or a directory with an __init__.py file, which we'll discuss later) and executes its code. The functions, classes, and variables defined in that file then become accessible through the module_name. prefix.

Understanding the Search Path: Where Python Looks for Modules

When you use import, Python searches for the module in a specific order:

1. The current directory (where your script is running)
2. Directories listed in the PYTHONPATH environment variable (if set)
3. Installation-dependent default directories (the standard library)

You can inspect the search path by examining the sys.path variable:

```python
import sys

print(sys.path)
```

This will print a list of directories that Python searches when importing modules.

Selective Imports: The from ... import ... Syntax

Sometimes, you only need to use a few specific functions or variables from a module. In these cases, you can use the from ... import ... syntax to import them directly into your namespace:

```python
from math import sqrt, pi

# Use sqrt() and pi directly without the module name
result = sqrt(16)
print(result)   # Output: 4.0
print(pi)       # Output: 3.141592653589793
```

This can make your code more concise, but it can also lead to naming conflicts if you import multiple functions with the same name from different modules. Be careful and be aware of which libraries you have imported.

Aliasing: Resolving Naming Conflicts with as

To avoid naming conflicts, you can rename modules or functions when you import them using the as keyword. This creates an alias, which is a different name that you can use to refer to the module or function:

```python
import math as m

# Use the alias "m" to access the math module
result = m.sqrt(16)
print(result)   # Output: 4.0

from math import sqrt as square_root

# Use the alias "square_root" to access the sqrt() function
result = square_root(16)
print(result)   # Output: 4.0
```

Aliasing can be a useful technique for resolving naming conflicts and making your code more readable. It increases code readability and maintainability.

Best Practices for Importing Modules: A Guide to Clarity and Maintainability

- **Keep imports at the top of your file:** This makes it easy to see which modules your code depends on.
- **Use the import statement for entire modules:** This is generally preferred over from ... import ... to avoid naming conflicts and improve code clarity.
- **Use aliases (as) when necessary to resolve naming conflicts:** This makes your code more readable and maintainable.
- **Avoid wildcard imports (from module import *):** This imports all the names from a module into your namespace, which can lead to naming conflicts and make your code harder to understand. Be specific about what you are importing.
- **Group your imports:** Separate standard library imports, third-party library imports, and local application imports into distinct groups with blank lines in between.

Important: Following these best practices will help you write code that is more readable, maintainable, and less prone to errors.

Beyond the Basics: Packages and Submodules (A Glimpse Ahead)

As your projects grow in complexity, you'll want to organize your code into packages. A package is a directory that contains multiple modules and a special file named __init__.py (which can be empty in recent versions of Python). Packages allow you to create a hierarchical structure for your code, making it easier to manage and reuse.

We'll explore packages in more detail later, but it's worth knowing that they exist and that they are a key part of Python's modularity system.

A Practical Example: Combining Modules for a Useful Task

Let's combine the math and random modules to create a function that generates a random number within a certain range and then calculates its square root:

```
import math
import random

def generate_random_square_root(min_value, max_value):
```

```
    """Generates a random number between min_value and
max_value and returns its square root."""
    random_number = random.randint(min_value, max_value)
    square_root = math.sqrt(random_number)
    return square_root

result = generate_random_square_root(1, 100)
print(f"The square root of a random number is: {result}")
```

This example demonstrates how to combine functions from different modules to perform a more complex task.

In Summary: Embrace the Power of Code Reuse

Importing modules is a fundamental skill for any Python programmer. It allows you to tap into a vast library of pre-written code, saving you time, effort, and potential reinvention of the wheel. By mastering the concepts and techniques presented in this section, you'll be well-equipped to leverage the power of the Python ecosystem and build more complex and sophisticated applications.

7.2: Adventures in the Standard Library: Discovering Hidden Gems

We've learned the mechanics of importing modules. Now, let's embark on an exciting exploration of some of the most useful and versatile modules that come bundled with Python, collectively known as the Standard Library. These modules are like a treasure trove of pre-built tools, ready to be used in your projects.

The Python Standard Library is vast and comprehensive, containing modules for everything from mathematics to networking to file handling. It's a testament to Python's "batteries included" philosophy, providing a rich set of tools that are ready to use right out of the box.

In this section, we'll explore a few of the most popular and widely used modules, showcasing their capabilities and inspiring you to delve deeper into the Standard Library on your own.

1. The math Module: Reaching for Mathematical Heights

The math module provides access to a wide range of mathematical functions, constants, and operations. It's your go-to module for performing calculations, working with numbers, and exploring mathematical concepts.

Key features and Real-World Use cases:

- **Basic Arithmetic:** You probably already know about sqrt(), but pow(x, y) handles exponents more generally.
- **Trigonometry:** sin(), cos(), tan(), and their inverse functions are essential for graphics, physics simulations, and signal processing.
- **Logarithmic Functions:** log(), log10(), and exp() are indispensable for scientific computing and data analysis.
- **Constants:** pi and e give you accurate representations of these fundamental mathematical constants.

Let's say you're building a program to calculate the distance between two points in a 2D plane. You can use the math module to perform the necessary calculations:

```python
import math

def distance(x1, y1, x2, y2):
    """Calculates the distance between two points in a 2D plane."""
    dx = x2 - x1
    dy = y2 - y1
    return math.sqrt(dx*dx + dy*dy)

distance1 = distance(0, 0, 3, 4) #5.0
print (f"Distance between two points in 2D plane = {distance1}")
```

2. The random Module: Embracing Uncertainty and Chance

The random module provides functions for generating random numbers, shuffling sequences, and making random choices. It's a powerful tool for simulations, games, and security applications.

Key features and Real-World Use cases:

- **Generating Random Numbers:** random() generates a random float between 0.0 and 1.0, randint(a, b) generates a random integer between a and b (inclusive), and uniform(a, b) generates a random float between a and b.

- **Choosing Random Elements:** choice(sequence) randomly selects an element from a sequence, and sample(population, k) randomly selects k unique elements from a population.
- **Shuffling Sequences:** shuffle(list) shuffles the elements of a list in place.

Let's build a simple dice rolling simulator:

```python
import random

def roll_dice():
    """Simulates rolling a six-sided die."""
    return random.randint(1, 6)

roll = roll_dice()
print(f"You rolled a {roll}")
```

3. The datetime Module: Navigating the Sands of Time

The datetime module provides classes for working with dates and times. It's your go-to module for storing, manipulating, and formatting date and time information.

Key features and Real-World Use cases:

- **Creating Date and Time Objects:** The date class represents a date (year, month, day), the time class represents a time (hour, minute, second, microsecond), and the datetime class represents a specific point in time.
- **Formatting Dates and Times:** The strftime() method allows you to format dates and times into strings according to a wide range of patterns.
- **Calculating Time Differences:** You can subtract date and datetime objects to calculate time differences.
- **Time Zones:** The timezone class allows you to work with time zones (but requires some more advanced knowledge).

Let's calculate how many days are left until New Year's Day:

```python
import datetime
```

```
today = datetime.date.today()
new_year = datetime.date(today.year + 1, 1, 1) #Calculate new
year's day of next year
days_left = (new_year - today).days #difference in days

print(f"There are {days_left} days left until New Year's
Day!")
```

4. The os Module: Interacting with Your Operating System

The os module provides functions for interacting with your operating system, including file system access, environment variables, and process management. It's your gateway to controlling your computer from within your Python programs.

Key features and Real-World Use cases:

- **File System Operations:** os.path.exists(path) checks if a file or directory exists, os.mkdir(path) creates a new directory, os.remove(path) deletes a file, and os.rename(old_path, new_path) renames a file or directory.
- **Environment Variables:** os.environ provides access to environment variables, which can be used to configure your programs.
- **Process Management:** os.system(command) executes a shell command. (It is more secure and modern to use the subprocess module, however).

Let's create a function that creates a directory if it doesn't already exist:

```
import os

def create_directory_if_not_exists(path):
    """Creates a directory if it doesn't already exist."""
    if not os.path.exists(path):
        os.makedirs(path)  # Use makedirs to create
intermediate directories
        print(f"Created directory: {path}")
    else:
        print(f"Directory already exists: {path}")

create_directory_if_not_exists("my_directory/subdirectory")
```

The os module can do far more than just create directories. It's a powerful interface to your operating system.

132

Your Challenge: Dive Deeper!

This is just a glimpse into the Python Standard Library. There are many other amazing modules waiting to be discovered! Take some time to explore the documentation and experiment with different modules. You'll be amazed at what you can accomplish with just a few lines of code.

Remember that a good programmer knows not just how to code, but also where to find the code they need.

In Summary: The Standard Library - Your Treasure Trove of Tools

The Python Standard Library is a rich and diverse collection of modules that provide solutions to a wide range of programming problems. By exploring the Standard Library, you can save time, improve the quality of your code, and gain a deeper understanding of Python's capabilities.

7.3: pip: Your Key to the Python Package Universe

We've explored the wonders of the Python Standard Library, but the real magic happens when you start leveraging the vast ecosystem of third-party packages. That's where pip, the Python package installer, comes in.

pip is your key to unlocking a universe of pre-built functionality, from web frameworks to data science libraries to machine learning toolkits. It allows you to easily install, manage, and uninstall packages from the Python Package Index (PyPI), a massive online repository of open-source Python software.

pip empowers you to extend Python's capabilities and build complex applications with ease.

Understanding pip: What It Does and Why It Matters

At its core, pip is a command-line tool that simplifies the process of installing and managing Python packages. It handles the complexities of downloading packages, resolving dependencies, and installing them in the correct locations.

Without pip, you would have to manually download packages, extract their contents, and copy them to the appropriate directories. This would be a tedious and error-prone process. pip automates this process, making it easy to add new functionality to your Python projects.

Basic pip Commands: Your Essential Toolkit

Here are the most common pip commands that you'll use on a regular basis:

- **pip install package_name:** Installs a package from PyPI. This is the command you'll use most often. Replace package_name with the name of the package you want to install (e.g., requests, numpy, django).

  Example:

  ```
  pip install requests
  ```

- **pip uninstall package_name:** Uninstalls a package. Use this to remove packages that you no longer need.

  Example:

  ```
  pip uninstall requests
  ```

- **pip list:** Lists all the packages that are currently installed in your environment. This is useful for seeing what packages you have available.

  Example:

  ```
  pip list
  ```

- **pip show package_name:** Displays information about a specific package, including its version, author, and dependencies.

  Example:

  ```
  pip show requests
  ```

- **pip freeze > requirements.txt:** Creates a requirements.txt file that lists all the packages installed in your environment, along with their versions. This is useful for creating reproducible environments (more on this later).

  Example:

  ```
  pip freeze > requirements.txt
  ```

- **pip install -r requirements.txt:** Installs all the packages listed in a requirements.txt file. This is used to recreate an environment based on a list of dependencies.

  Example:

  ```
  pip install -r requirements.txt
  ```

Step-by-Step Guide to Installing a Package: A Practical Example

Let's walk through the process of installing the requests package, a popular library for making HTTP requests:

1. **Open a Terminal or Command Prompt:**
2. **Ensure pip is Up to Date (Important!)** While it often comes with Python, making sure pip is the newest version will help avoid installation issues. Upgrade with:

   ```
   pip install --upgrade pip
   ```

3. **Run the pip install Command:**

   ```
   pip install requests
   ```

   pip will download the requests package and any dependencies it requires from PyPI and install them in your Python environment.

4. **Verify the Installation:**

You can verify that the package has been installed successfully by running the following command:

```
pip show requests
```

This will display information about the requests package, including its version and location.

5. **Use the Package in Your Code:**

   Now that the package is installed, you can import it into your Python code and use its functions and classes:

```
import requests

response = requests.get("https://www.example.com")
print(response.status_code)  # Output: 200
print(response.content)
```

Dependency Management: Keeping Your Projects Consistent

As your projects grow in complexity, you'll likely use many different packages. Managing these dependencies can become challenging, especially when you're working on multiple projects that require different versions of the same packages.

Virtual environments (which we'll cover in the next section) are essential for managing dependencies and ensuring that your projects are reproducible.

Creating a requirements.txt File: Capturing Your Dependencies

A requirements.txt file is a simple text file that lists all the packages that are required by your project, along with their versions. This file allows you to easily recreate the environment for your project on a different machine or at a later time.

To create a requirements.txt file, run the following command in your project's root directory:

```
pip freeze > requirements.txt
```

This command will generate a requirements.txt file that lists all the packages installed in your current environment, along with their versions.

Installing Packages from a requirements.txt File: Recreating Your Environment

To install the packages listed in a requirements.txt file, run the following command:

```
pip install -r requirements.txt
```

This command will install all the packages listed in the requirements.txt file, along with their specified versions.

Common pip Problems and How to Solve Them

- **pip command not found:** This usually means that pip is not installed or not in your system's PATH. Make sure you have Python installed correctly and that pip is included.
- **"Requirement already satisfied":** This means that the package is already installed in your environment. If you want to reinstall it, you can use the --force-reinstall option.
- **"Could not find a version that satisfies the requirement":** This usually means that there's a conflict between the package you're trying to install and other packages that are already installed. Try creating a virtual environment to isolate your dependencies.
- **Permission errors:** On some systems, you might need to use sudo to install packages globally. However, it's generally better to use virtual environments instead of installing packages globally.

A Practical Example: Automating Package Installation

Let's create a script that automates the process of installing packages from a requirements.txt file:

```python
import subprocess

def install_requirements(requirements_file):
    """Installs packages from a requirements.txt file."""
    try:
        subprocess.check_call(["pip", "install", "-r",
requirements_file]) #Executes as if at command line, throwing
error if anything fails
```

```
        print(f"Successfully installed packages from
{requirements_file}")
    except FileNotFoundError:
        print(f"Error: The requirements file
'{requirements_file}' was not found.")
    except subprocess.CalledProcessError as e:
        print(f"Error: Failed to install packages. {e}")

install_requirements("requirements.txt")
```

This script uses the subprocess module to execute the pip install -r requirements.txt command. It also includes error handling to catch potential exceptions.

In Summary: Embrace pip and Unlock Python's Potential

pip is your key to unlocking the full potential of the Python ecosystem. By mastering pip and using virtual environments, you can easily install, manage, and isolate your project dependencies, ensuring that your code is reproducible and reliable.

7.4: Virtual Environments: Your Island of Python Sanity

We've learned how to install packages using pip, unlocking a vast ecosystem of functionality. But as you start working on multiple projects, a problem arises: different projects may require different versions of the *same* packages. Installing packages globally can lead to conflicts and break your code.

That's where virtual environments come to the rescue. They are the key to Python sanity, the tool that allows you to create isolated environments for each of your projects.

Think of virtual environments as separate containers for your Python projects, each with its own set of dependencies. It's like having multiple versions of Python installed on your computer, each tailored to a specific project.

Why Virtual Environments are Essential: The Problems They Solve

Virtual environments address several critical problems in Python development:

- **Dependency Conflicts:** Different projects might require different versions of the same packages. Installing packages globally can lead to conflicts, where one project's dependencies break another project's dependencies.
- **Reproducibility:** If you don't use virtual environments, it can be difficult to recreate the exact environment that your project was developed in. This can make it hard to share your code with others or deploy it to a production server.
- **Global Pollution:** Installing packages globally can pollute your system's Python installation with unnecessary dependencies. This can make your system more complex and harder to maintain.
- **Permissions Issues:** Installing packages globally might require administrative privileges (e.g., using sudo on Linux/macOS). This can be inconvenient and potentially insecure.

Virtual environments solve all of these problems by creating isolated environments for each of your projects, ensuring that they have their own set of dependencies and that they don't interfere with each other.

The venv Module: Your Tool for Creating Virtual Environments

Python 3 comes with the venv module, a lightweight and easy-to-use tool for creating virtual environments.

Step-by-Step Guide to Creating and Using a Virtual Environment

Let's walk through the process of creating and using a virtual environment:

1. **Choose a Project Directory:**

   Navigate to the directory where you want to create your project.

   ```
   cd my_project
   ```

2. **Create a Virtual Environment:**

   Use the python -m venv command to create a new virtual environment in a subdirectory named venv (you can choose any name you like):

   ```
   python -m venv venv
   ```

This will create a new directory named venv (or whatever name you chose) that contains the virtual environment.

3. **Activate the Virtual Environment:**

To activate the virtual environment, you need to run a script that sets up the environment variables. The script is located in the "venv/bin" directory (on macOS/Linux) or the "venv\Scripts" directory (on Windows).

- o **macOS/Linux:**

```
source venv/bin/activate
```

- o **Windows:**

```
venv\Scripts\activate
```

When the virtual environment is activated, your terminal prompt will change to indicate that you're working within the environment. For example, you might see (venv) at the beginning of your prompt.

4. **Install Packages within the Virtual Environment:**

Once the virtual environment is activated, you can install packages using pip as usual:

```
pip install requests
```

The packages will be installed in the virtual environment, and they won't affect any other Python installations on your system.

5. **Work on Your Project:**

Now that you've activated the virtual environment and installed the necessary packages, you can start working on your project.

6. **Deactivate the Virtual Environment:**

   When you're finished working on your project, you can deactivate the virtual environment by running the deactivate command:

   ```
   deactivate
   ```

   Your terminal prompt will return to normal, indicating that you're no longer working within the virtual environment.

A Practical Analogy: The Sandbox

Think of a virtual environment as a sandbox for your Python projects. Each project gets its own sandbox, where it can play with its own set of toys (packages) without affecting any other sandboxes. This prevents conflicts and ensures that each project can have its own unique set of dependencies.

Tips for Working with Virtual Environments

- **Always use virtual environments:** Make it a habit to create a virtual environment for every Python project you work on.
- **Name your virtual environments consistently:** Choose a naming convention and stick to it (e.g., venv, .venv, env).
- **Store your virtual environments in a dedicated directory:** This makes it easier to manage your virtual environments.
- **Exclude your virtual environment directory from version control:** Add the virtual environment directory (e.g., venv) to your .gitignore file to prevent it from being tracked by Git. This is important because virtual environments contain platform-specific files that should not be shared across different operating systems.

In Summary: Embrace Virtual Environments for Sanity and Reliability

Virtual environments are an essential tool for any serious Python developer. They allow you to isolate your project dependencies, prevent conflicts, and ensure that your projects are reproducible. By mastering virtual environments, you'll be able to write more reliable, maintainable, and scalable Python code.

Chapter 8: Project: Building a Simple Tool: Putting Your Skills to the Test

Welcome to Chapter 8! We've covered a lot of ground, learning about variables, data types, control flow, functions, modules, and packages. Now, it's time to put those skills to the test by building a simple tool from scratch.

This chapter is all about *doing*. It's about taking the theoretical knowledge you've acquired and applying it to a real-world problem. We'll guide you through the entire process, from defining the project scope to testing and refining the final product.

Think of this as your apprenticeship. It is time to learn by doing and practicing and becoming a better programmer.

Choosing a Project: To-Do List, Unit Converter, or...?

For this chapter, we'll focus on building a command-line to-do list application. It's a classic project that's simple enough to be completed in a reasonable amount of time, but complex enough to illustrate many important programming concepts.

However, you're welcome to choose a different project if you prefer. Some other ideas include:

- **Unit Converter:** Convert between different units of measurement (e.g., Celsius to Fahrenheit, miles to kilometers).
- **Simple Calculator:** Perform basic arithmetic operations.
- **Password Generator:** Generate random passwords.
- **Basic Quiz:** Ask the user a series of questions and track their score.

No matter which project you choose, the steps in this chapter will be applicable.

8.1: Defining the Project Scope: Drawing the Boundaries of Your Creation

Before you write a single line of code, before you even *think* about code, you need to answer one fundamental question: **What will this project actually do?**

That's what defining the project scope is all about. It's about setting clear boundaries for your project, defining its intended functionality, and explicitly stating what it *will* and *will not* do. It is one of the most important parts of creating a successful project.

Think of it as drawing a map *before* you start your journey. Without a map, you're likely to get lost, wander aimlessly, and never reach your destination.

Why Scope Matters: Avoiding the Abyss of Scope Creep

Defining the project scope is not just a formality; it's a crucial risk management strategy. It helps you avoid a phenomenon known as *scope creep*, which is the tendency for projects to gradually expand beyond their original scope, adding new features and requirements along the way.

Scope creep is a project killer. It can lead to:

- **Delays:** As the scope expands, the project takes longer to complete.
- **Increased Costs:** More features mean more development effort, which translates to higher costs.
- **Reduced Quality:** As the project becomes more complex, it becomes harder to test and maintain, leading to lower quality.
- **Frustration:** Scope creep can be frustrating for everyone involved, as the project becomes a moving target.

By defining a clear and realistic scope upfront, you can prevent scope creep and keep your project on track.

The Art of Defining Scope: A Practical Approach

Defining the project scope is an iterative process. It involves brainstorming, prioritizing, and making tough decisions about what to include and what to exclude.

Here's a practical approach to defining scope:

1. **Identify the Core Problem:** What problem are you trying to solve with this project? Be specific. A good problem statement is focused and measurable.
2. **Brainstorm Features:** List all the features that you *could* potentially include in the project. Don't worry about feasibility at this stage; just get all your ideas down on paper.
3. **Prioritize Features:** Rank the features in terms of their importance and value. Which features are absolutely essential for solving the core problem? Which features are nice-to-haves that could be added later?
4. **Define the Minimum Viable Product (MVP):** Identify the smallest set of features that would deliver a functional and valuable product. This is your MVP. The MVP should address the core problem and provide a foundation for future development.
5. **Explicitly Exclude Features:** List any features that you are explicitly excluding from the project. This helps to set clear boundaries and prevent scope creep.
6. **Document Your Scope:** Write down the project scope in a clear and concise document. This document should be shared with all stakeholders to ensure that everyone is on the same page.

A Template for Defining Project Scope

Here's a template that you can use to document your project scope:

- **Project Name:** (The name of your project)
- **Problem Statement:** (A clear and concise description of the problem you're trying to solve)
- **Goals:** (What you're hoping to achieve with this project)
- **Minimum Viable Product (MVP):** (The core features that will be included in the first release)
  - Feature 1
  - Feature 2
  - Feature 3
- **Out of Scope:** (Features that will *not* be included in the first release)
  - Feature A
  - Feature B
  - Feature C

Applying the Template to the To-Do List Project

Let's apply this template to our To-Do List project:

- **Project Name:** To-Do List Application
- **Problem Statement:** Users need a simple way to manage their tasks and track their progress.
- **Goals:** To create a command-line application that allows users to add, view, mark as completed, and delete tasks from a to-do list.
- **Minimum Viable Product (MVP):**
  - Add tasks to the to-do list.
  - View the tasks in the to-do list.
  - Mark tasks as completed.
  - Delete tasks from the to-do list.
  - Persist the to-do list to a file so it's saved between program runs.
- **Out of Scope:**
  - Graphical user interface (GUI).
  - Support for multiple users.
  - Complex task management features (e.g., priorities, due dates, categories).
  - Cloud synchronization

The Importance of "No": Learning to Say No to Scope Creep

One of the most important skills for a software developer is the ability to say "no" to new feature requests that are outside the scope of the project. It can be tempting to add new features, but it's important to remember that every new feature adds complexity and increases the risk of scope creep.

Learn to politely but firmly decline requests that are outside the agreed-upon scope. Explain that those features can be considered for future releases, but that they are not part of the current project.

In Summary: Start Small, Stay Focused, and Deliver Value

Defining the project scope is a crucial step in any software development project. By clearly defining what the project will do and what it won't do, you can prevent scope creep, stay focused on the core problem, and deliver a valuable product to your users. Remember, it's better to deliver a small, well-defined project on time than a large, complex project that's late, over budget, and of poor quality.

8.2: Designing the Program Structure: From Vision to Blueprint

With the project scope clearly defined, it's time to move from the abstract to the concrete. It's time to design the program structure – to create a blueprint for how your application will work.

This is where you decide how to organize your code, what data structures to use, what functions to define, and how those functions will interact with each other. A well-designed program structure is essential for creating code that is easy to understand, maintain, and extend.

Think of it as designing the architecture of a building. You need to consider the different rooms, their purpose, and how they connect to each other. A well-designed building is both functional and aesthetically pleasing.

Why Program Structure Matters: The Foundation for Success

A well-designed program structure is crucial for several reasons:

- **Readability:** A clear and logical structure makes your code easier to read and understand. This is especially important when you're working on a team or when you need to maintain the code later.
- **Maintainability:** A modular structure makes your code easier to maintain. You can make changes to one part of the code without affecting other parts.
- **Testability:** A well-structured program is easier to test. You can test individual components in isolation, making it easier to find and fix bugs.
- **Reusability:** A modular structure promotes code reuse. You can reuse components in other projects, saving time and effort.

Key Elements of Program Design: Data Structures, Functions, and Flow

Designing a program structure involves making decisions about three key elements:

1. **Data Structures:** Choosing the appropriate data structures to store and manage your data.
2. **Functions:** Defining the functions that will perform specific tasks in your program.

3. **Program Flow:** Planning the overall flow of execution, including how the different functions will be called and how the program will interact with the user.

1. Choosing the Right Data Structures: Organizing Your Information

Data structures are the containers that hold your program's data. Choosing the right data structures is crucial for performance and efficiency.

For our To-Do List project, we need a way to store the tasks. A list of dictionaries is a good choice because:

- Lists are ordered: We want to maintain the order in which the tasks were added.
- Dictionaries allow us to store multiple pieces of information about each task (description and completion status).

So, our data structure will look like this:

```
tasks = [
{"task": "Grocery Shopping", "completed": False},
{"task": "Laundry", "completed": True},
{"task": "Pay Bills", "completed": False}
]
```

2. Defining Function Responsibilities: Small, Focused Tasks

Functions should be small, self-contained units that perform a specific task. Each function should have a clear purpose and a well-defined interface (arguments and return values).

For our To-Do List project, let's define the following functions:

- add_task(tasks, task_description): Adds a new task to the tasks list.
- view_tasks(tasks): Displays the tasks in the tasks list.
- mark_completed(tasks, task_index): Marks the task at the specified index in the tasks list as completed.
- delete_task(tasks, task_index): Deletes the task at the specified index from the tasks list.
- load_tasks(): Loads tasks from a file (e.g., tasks.json).
- save_tasks(tasks): Saves tasks to a file (e.g., tasks.json).

- get_user_choice(): Display the menu and get the user's selected choice.

Notice that each function has a clear and specific responsibility. This makes the code easier to read, test, and maintain.

3. Planning the Program Flow: Connecting the Pieces

The program flow defines how the different functions will be called and how the program will interact with the user. A well-planned program flow makes the application easy to use and understand.

For our To-Do List project, let's define the following program flow:

1. Load tasks from the file (if it exists).
2. Display the menu of options to the user.
3. Get the user's choice.
4. Call the appropriate function based on the user's choice.
5. Repeat steps 2-4 until the user chooses to quit.
6. Save tasks to the file.

This flow is easy to understand and provides a logical progression for the user.

From Design to Code: Implementing the Structure

Let's translate our design into code (this is a snippet; see full code in the previous section). Note how each element maps to our design:

```python
    import json

#Functions
def add_task(tasks, task):
    tasks.append({"task": task, "completed": False})

def load_tasks():
    #Load from JSON

def main(): #Main Program flow
    tasks = load_tasks()

    while True:
        #Print choices
        choice = input()
```

```
if choice == "1":
    add_task(tasks, input())
```

A Visual Aid: Flowcharts or Diagrams (Optional)

For more complex projects, it can be helpful to create a flowchart or diagram to visualize the program structure and flow. Tools like draw.io or Lucidchart can be used to create these diagrams. This can be helpful for communicating the design to other developers or for clarifying your own understanding.

In Summary: Plan Before You Build, Building on a Solid Foundation

Designing the program structure is a critical step in the software development process. By carefully considering data structures, function responsibilities, and program flow, you can create code that is easier to understand, maintain, test, and reuse. Remember to plan before you build, and build on a solid foundation.

8.3: Implementing the Core Logic: The Code Comes to Life

With the project scope defined and the program structure designed, it's time to translate our blueprint into reality. This is where the code comes to life, where we bring our vision to fruition. This section is about the art of implementation: writing clean, efficient, and well-documented code that accurately reflects our design.

This is the "doing" part, but it's not just about typing code; it's about thinking carefully about each line, ensuring that it's correct, efficient, and easy to understand.

From Design to Implementation: A Function-by-Function Journey

We'll proceed function by function, carefully implementing each component of our To-Do List application. Remember, our goal is not just to make the code *work*, but to make it *well-written* code.

1. The add_task(tasks, task_description) Function: Adding New Tasks

This function is responsible for adding new tasks to the to-do list. It takes the tasks list (our data structure) and the task description as input and adds a new dictionary representing the task to the list.

```python
def add_task(tasks, task_description):
    """Adds a new task to the to-do list.

    Args:
        tasks: The list of tasks (list of dictionaries).
        task_description: The description of the task
(string).
    """
    tasks.append({"task": task_description, "completed":
False})
    print(f"Task '{task_description}' added.")
```

Key Considerations:

- **Docstring:** The function has a clear and concise docstring that explains what it does and what arguments it takes.
- **Data Structure:** We're using a dictionary to represent each task, with keys for "task" (the description) and "completed" (a boolean indicating whether the task is done).
- **Appending to the List:** We're using the append() method to add the new task to the end of the tasks list, maintaining the order in which the tasks were added.
- **Confirmation Message:** The function prints a confirmation message to the console, providing feedback to the user.

2. The view_tasks(tasks) Function: Displaying the To-Do List

This function displays the tasks in the to-do list, showing their description and completion status.

```python
def view_tasks(tasks):
    """Displays the tasks in the to-do list.

    Args:
        tasks: The list of tasks (list of dictionaries).
    """
    if not tasks:
        print("No tasks in the to-do list.")
        return

    for index, task in enumerate(tasks):
        status = "[x]" if task["completed"] else "[ ]"
        print(f"{index + 1}. {status} {task['task']}")
```

Key Considerations:

- **Handling Empty List:** The function checks if the tasks list is empty and prints a message if it is.
- **enumerate():** We're using the enumerate() function to iterate over the tasks list and get both the index and the value of each task.
- **Completion Status:** We're using a conditional expression to display the completion status as "[x]" or "[ ]".
- **User-Friendly Output:** We're formatting the output to be easy to read and understand.

3. The mark_completed(tasks, task_index) Function: Changing Task Status

This function marks a task as completed, changing its "completed" status to True.

```python
def mark_completed(tasks, task_index):
    """Marks a task as completed.

    Args:
        tasks: The list of tasks (list of dictionaries).
        task_index: The index of the task to mark as
completed (string).
    """
    try:
        task_index = int(task_index) - 1 #Adjusts it to the
list's 0 based index
        if 0 <= task_index < len(tasks):
            tasks[task_index]["completed"] = True
            print(f"Task '{tasks[task_index]['task']}' marked
as completed.")
        else:
            print("Invalid task number.")
    except ValueError:
        print("Invalid task number.")
```

Key Considerations:

- **Error Handling:** We're using a try-except block to handle potential ValueError exceptions if the user enters an invalid task number.
- **Input Validation:** We're checking if the task index is within the valid range of the tasks list.

- **Modifying the Data Structure:** We're directly modifying the "completed" key of the task dictionary.
- **Index Shifting** Note that task lists display as starting from one, so we need to adjust our user's input to index correctly.

4. The delete_task(tasks, task_index) Function: Removing Tasks

This function deletes a task from the to-do list.

```python
    def delete_task(tasks, task_index):
    """Deletes a task from the to-do list.

    Args:
        tasks: The list of tasks (list of dictionaries).
        task_index: The index of the task to delete (string).
    """
    try:
        task_index = int(task_index) - 1
        if 0 <= task_index < len(tasks):
            deleted_task = tasks.pop(task_index)
            print(f"Task '{deleted_task['task']}' deleted.")
        else:
            print("Invalid task number.")
    except ValueError:
        print("Invalid task number.")
```

Key Considerations:

- **Error Handling:** We're using a try-except block to handle potential ValueError exceptions.
- **Input Validation:** We're checking if the task index is within the valid range of the tasks list.
- **pop() Method:** We're using the pop() method to remove the task from the list and get its value.
- **Index Shifting** As in the mark_completed function, user input must be adjusted to correct index.

5. The load_tasks() Function: Bringing in Existing Data

This function loads tasks from a JSON file, allowing the to-do list to persist between program runs.

```python
    import json
```

152

```
def load_tasks():
    """Loads tasks from a JSON file."""
    try:
        with open("tasks.json", "r", encoding = "utf-8") as
file:
            tasks = json.load(file)
        print("Tasks loaded from tasks.json")
        return tasks
    except FileNotFoundError:
        print("No tasks found. Starting with an empty to-do
list.")
        return []
    except json.JSONDecodeError:
        print("Error loading JSON data")
        return [] #Return empty array
```

Key Considerations:

- **JSON Module:** We're using the json module to read JSON data from the file.
- **with Statement:** We're using the with statement to ensure that the file is closed properly.
- **Error Handling:** We're handling potential FileNotFoundError exceptions if the file doesn't exist, and json.JSONDecodeError exceptions for bad formatting.
- **Returning a Value:** The function returns the list of tasks that were loaded from the file (or an empty list if the file doesn't exist or contains bad data).

6. The save_tasks() Function: Saving Progress

This function saves the tasks to a JSON file, ensuring that the to-do list is persisted between program runs.

```
def save_tasks(tasks):
    """Saves tasks to a JSON file."""
    try:
        with open("tasks.json", "w", encoding = "utf-8") as
file:
            json.dump(tasks, file)
        print("Tasks saved to tasks.json")
    except Exception as e:
        print (f"Unable to save file {e}")
```

Key Considerations:

- **JSON Module:** We're using the json module to write JSON data to the file.
- **with Statement:** We're using the with statement to ensure that the file is closed properly.
- **Error Handling:** A catch-all for problems with the file saving process, to avoid data loss.

Beyond the Code: The Importance of Clear Intent

As you write your code, always strive to make your intent clear. Use descriptive variable names, write concise comments, and follow consistent code style guidelines. This will make your code easier to read, understand, and maintain.

In Summary: Translate Design into Functional Code

Implementing the core logic is the heart of any software project. By carefully translating your design into clean, efficient, and well-documented code, you can bring your vision to life and create a valuable tool for your users.

End of Section 8.3

Key Improvements:

- **Presented implementation as a translation of design:** Emphasized the link between planning and coding.
- **Walked through each function, explaining the rationale behind the code:** Provided a deep dive into the thought process.
- **Highlighted key considerations for each function:** Emphasized data structures, error handling, and code style.
- **Encouraged clear intent:** Advocated for descriptive names, comments, and consistent style.
- **Maintained a conversational and engaging tone:** Kept the language accessible and enthusiastic.

Is this a good approach to guiding the reader through the code implementation phase? Should we make more changes?

8.4: Adding User Input and Output: Talking to Your Users

With the core logic of our To-Do List application in place, it's time to add the user interface. In this case, it's a command-line interface (CLI). This is what allows the user to interact with our program, to tell it what to do, and to see the results.

A well-designed user interface is crucial for making your application easy to use and understand. Even the most powerful and feature-rich program is useless if users can't figure out how to use it.

Think of the user interface as a conversation between your program and the user. You want to make that conversation as clear, concise, and intuitive as possible.

The main() Function: Orchestrating the Interaction

The main() function is the heart of our CLI. It's responsible for presenting the menu of options to the user, getting their input, and calling the appropriate functions based on their choice.

```python
def main():
    """Main function to run the to-do list application."""
    tasks = load_tasks() #Load existing tasks

    while True:
        print("\nTo-Do List Application")
        print("1. Add task")
        print("2. View tasks")
        print("3. Mark task as completed")
        print("4. Delete task")
        print("5. Save and Quit")

        choice = input("Enter your choice: ")

        if choice == "1":
            task = input("Enter the task: ")
            add_task(tasks, task)
        elif choice == "2":
            view_tasks(tasks)
        elif choice == "3":
            task_number = input("Enter the task number to mark as completed: ")
            mark_completed(tasks, task_number)
        elif choice == "4":
```

```
        task_number = input("Enter the task number to
delete: ")
        delete_task(tasks, task_number)
    elif choice == "5":
        save_tasks(tasks)
        break
    else:
        print("Invalid choice. Please try again.")

if __name__ == "__main__": #This code will only run when run
as a top-level script
    main()
```

Let's break down the key elements of this function:

- **The while True Loop:** This creates an infinite loop that continues until the user chooses to quit (by entering "5").
- **The Menu:** The print() statements display the menu of options to the user. The \n characters add blank lines to make the menu more readable.
- **The input() Function:** This prompts the user to enter their choice. The input() function always returns a string.
- **The if-elif-else Statement:** This checks the user's choice and calls the appropriate function.
- **Error Handling:** The else block handles the case where the user enters an invalid choice.
- **The break Statement:** This exits the loop when the user chooses to quit.
- **Calling load_tasks at startup** Immediately load persistent storage.
- **Calling save_tasks on exit.** Save data on the way out to save user progress.

Guiding the User: Clear Prompts and Instructions

The key to a good user interface is to provide clear prompts and instructions. Tell the user exactly what you expect them to do.

- Use descriptive prompts for the input() function:

```
    task = input("Enter the task: ")  # Clear and concise
prompt
```

- Provide feedback to the user after they perform an action:

```
print(f"Task '{task}' added.")  # Confirmation message
```

- Handle errors gracefully and provide informative error messages:

```
print("Invalid choice. Please try again.")  # Error
message
```

Handling Invalid Input: Preventing Crashes and Frustration

Users don't always enter the input that you expect. It's important to handle invalid input gracefully to prevent your program from crashing or producing unexpected results.

- **Use try-except blocks to handle potential errors:**

```
try:
    task_index = int(task_number)
    # ...
except ValueError:
    print("Invalid task number.")
```

- **Validate user input:**

```
if 0 <= task_index < len(tasks):
    # ..
else:
    print ("Please enter a number between 1 and " +
str(len(tasks)))
```

The Power of Feedback: Keeping the User Informed

Providing feedback to the user is essential for making your application feel responsive and intuitive. Let the user know what's happening, whether their actions were successful, and if there were any errors.

- **Confirmation Messages:** After the user adds a task, marks it as complete, or deletes it, print a confirmation message to let them know that the action was successful.
- **Error Messages:** If the user enters invalid input or if an error occurs, print an informative error message that explains what went wrong and how to fix it.

157

- **Status Updates:** If the program is performing a long-running task (e.g., loading or saving a large file), provide status updates to let the user know that the program is still working.

Beyond the Basics: Improving the User Experience

Here are some additional tips for improving the user experience:

- **Use color and formatting to make the output more readable:** You can use libraries like colorama to add color to your terminal output.
- **Provide a help command:** Allow the user to type "help" to see a list of available commands and their usage.
- **Implement tab completion:** Allow the user to press the Tab key to automatically complete commands or filenames.
- **Use a more sophisticated command-line interface library:** Libraries like argparse and click provide more advanced features for creating command-line interfaces.

In Summary: Create a Conversation, Not a Monologue

Adding user input and output is essential for making your application interactive and user-friendly. By providing clear prompts, handling invalid input gracefully, and providing informative feedback, you can create a user interface that is a pleasure to use. Remember, it's not just about telling the computer what to do; it's about creating a conversation between your program and the user.

8.5: Testing and Refining the Tool: The Journey to Excellence

We've built our To-Do List application, line by line, from design to implementation. But the journey doesn't end there. In fact, in many ways, it's just beginning. The real challenge is to transform our functional code into a *polished* product that is reliable, user-friendly, and maintainable. That's where testing and refinement come in.

Testing and refinement are not just afterthoughts; they're integral parts of the software development process. They're about identifying and fixing bugs, improving the user experience, and making your code the best it can be.

Think of testing and refinement as sanding and polishing a piece of furniture. You start with a rough-hewn piece of wood, and gradually transform it into a smooth, elegant, and functional object.

The Importance of Testing: Finding the Flaws

Testing is the process of verifying that your code works as expected and that it meets the requirements defined in the project scope. It's about finding the flaws before your users do.

There are several types of testing that you can perform:

- **Unit Testing:** Testing individual functions or components in isolation. This helps to identify bugs early in the development process. While we won't introduce the complexities of an automated unit testing framework, you can simply run the functions one by one with varying inputs to check functionality.
- **Integration Testing:** Testing how different components of the system work together. This helps to identify bugs that arise from interactions between different parts of the code.
- **System Testing:** Testing the entire system as a whole. This helps to verify that the system meets all of the requirements.
- **User Acceptance Testing (UAT):** Testing the system from the perspective of the end user. This helps to ensure that the system is usable and meets the needs of the users.

For our To-Do List project, we'll focus on system testing and user acceptance testing.

Testing Strategies: A Multifaceted Approach

Here are some strategies for testing our To-Do List application:

1. **Functional Testing:** Test all the features of the application to make sure that they work as expected.
   - Can you add tasks to the to-do list?
   - Can you view the tasks in the to-do list?
   - Can you mark tasks as completed?
   - Can you delete tasks from the to-do list?
   - Are the tasks saved to a file?
   - Are the tasks loaded from the file when the application starts?

159

2. **Input Validation Testing:** Test how the application handles invalid input.
   o What happens if you enter a non-numeric value for the task number?
   o What happens if you enter a task number that is out of range?
   o What happens if the config file is corrupted?
3. **Edge Case Testing:** Test the application with edge cases, such as empty lists or very long task descriptions.
4. **User Acceptance Testing (UAT):** Ask someone else to use the application and provide feedback. This can help you identify usability issues that you might have missed.

Refinement Strategies: Turning Good Code into Great Code

Refinement is the process of improving the code based on the results of testing. It's about making the code more reliable, user-friendly, and maintainable.

Here are some strategies for refining our To-Do List application:

1. **Improve Error Handling:** Add more robust error handling to prevent the application from crashing or producing unexpected results. Think about what could go wrong and add code to handle those situations gracefully.
   o What if the tasks.json file is corrupted, and cannot be loaded?
   o What if the user does not have permissions to write to the tasks.json file?
2. **Enhance the User Interface:** Make the user interface more intuitive and user-friendly.
   o Add color and formatting to the output to make it easier to read.
   o Provide more informative prompts and instructions.
   o Add a help command that lists all the available options.
3. **Optimize the Code:** Make the code more efficient and performant. This might involve using more efficient data structures or algorithms.
4. **Add New Features (Carefully!):** Only add new features if they are within the scope of the project and if they provide significant value to the user. Be careful about scope creep!

Seeking Feedback: The Power of Outside Perspectives

One of the most valuable things you can do is to get feedback from other people. Ask friends, family members, or colleagues to use your application and provide their honest feedback. They might identify issues that you missed or suggest improvements that you hadn't thought of.

Be open to feedback, even if it's critical. Remember that the goal is to make your application the best it can be.

The Iterative Cycle: Test, Refine, Repeat

Testing and refinement are not one-time activities; they're an iterative cycle. You should test your code frequently, identify areas for improvement, and then refine the code. Then, test again, and repeat the process.

This iterative cycle is essential for creating high-quality software.

In Summary: The Pursuit of Excellence is Ongoing

Testing and refinement are essential steps in the software development process. By embracing a mindset of continuous improvement, you can transform your functional code into a polished product that is reliable, user-friendly, and maintainable. Remember that the journey to excellence is ongoing, and there's always room for improvement.

Chapter 9: Project: Data Analysis with Python: Unveiling Insights from Data

Welcome to Chapter 9! In the previous chapter, we built a simple tool to manage to-do lists. Now, we'll take our skills to the next level and explore the fascinating world of data analysis. We will use Python to process, analyze, and visualize data.

This chapter is all about extracting meaning from data. It's about taking raw information and transforming it into insights that can inform decisions, solve problems, and tell stories. We will be learning how to use Python to do what the best analysts are already doing: making smart data-driven choices.

Choosing a Dataset: A Real-World Example

For this chapter, we'll work with a dataset of sales data. You can find many sample datasets online, or you can create your own. A good starting point could be a CSV file with data such as transaction date, product name, quantity sold, and price.

9.1: CSV Files: The Ubiquitous Language of Data

In the world of data analysis, you'll encounter a bewildering variety of file formats, from complex databases to proprietary binary files. But amidst this diversity, one format stands out for its simplicity, portability, and widespread adoption: the CSV file.

CSV, short for Comma Separated Values, is a plain text format used to store tabular data. Each row in the file represents a record, and each column represents a field. The values in each row are separated by commas (or, less commonly, other delimiters).

Think of CSV files as the lingua franca of data. They're a common language that can be easily understood by a wide range of applications, making them an ideal format for exchanging data between systems.

Why CSV Endures: A Blend of Simplicity and Versatility

Despite their simplicity, CSV files have proven remarkably resilient and continue to be a mainstay in data management and analysis. Here's why:

- **Human-Readable and Editable:** CSV files are plain text, meaning you can open them with any text editor and easily read and modify the data. This is invaluable for quick inspections, manual corrections, and debugging.
- **Platform-Independent:** CSV files can be created and processed on any operating system, making them ideal for sharing data across different platforms.
- **Wide Compatibility:** CSV is supported by a vast range of applications, including spreadsheets, databases, programming languages, and data analysis tools.
- **Easy to Generate and Parse:** CSV files are relatively easy to generate programmatically, and they can be parsed efficiently with simple code.

These factors combine to make CSV files a versatile and convenient choice for many data-related tasks.

Anatomy of a CSV File: Dissecting the Structure

Let's examine the structure of a typical CSV file:

```
    Header Row,Defines the Columns
"Field 1","Field 2","Field 3"
"Value 1","Value 2","Value 3"
"Value 4","Value 5","Value 6"
```

Key components:

- **Header Row (Optional):** The first row often contains the names of the columns or fields. This is not strictly required, but it's highly recommended, as it makes the data much easier to understand.
- **Data Rows:** Each subsequent row represents a record, with the values for each field separated by a delimiter (usually a comma).
- **Delimiter:** The character used to separate the values in each row. The most common delimiter is a comma (,), but other delimiters, such as tabs (\t), semicolons (;), or pipes (|), are also used.
- **Quoting:** Values are often enclosed in double quotes (") to handle fields that contain commas or other special characters. Quoting ensures that the values are parsed correctly.

- **Newline Character:** Each row is typically terminated with a newline character (\n or \r\n, depending on the operating system).

CSV Variations: Navigating the Delimiter Jungle

While the basic CSV format is simple, there are many variations in how CSV files are structured. Some common variations include:

- **Different Delimiters:** Instead of commas, some CSV files use tabs, semicolons, or other characters as delimiters. These are often referred to as "TSV" (Tab Separated Values) or "DSV" (Delimiter Separated Values) files.
- **Different Quote Characters:** Some CSV files use different quote characters, such as single quotes (').
- **Escaping:** Different techniques for escaping special characters within quoted fields. Some files use backslashes (), while others use double quotes ("").
- **Line Endings:** Different operating systems use different line ending conventions (e.g., \n on Linux/macOS, \r\n on Windows).

It's important to be aware of these variations and to handle them appropriately when parsing CSV files.

Limitations of CSV: Knowing the Trade-offs

While CSV files are versatile, they also have some limitations:

- **No Data Types:** All values are stored as strings. You need to explicitly convert them to the appropriate data types (e.g., integers, floats) when parsing the file.
- **No Metadata:** CSV files don't store any metadata about the data, such as column names, data types, or units of measurement. This information needs to be stored separately.
- **Limited Structure:** CSV files are primarily designed for storing tabular data. They are not well-suited for storing hierarchical or complex data structures.
- **Handling of Special Characters:** Complicated due to delimiters and quoting.
- **No Standard:** While broadly used, there's no strict CSV "standard," leading to variations.

A Practical Example: Inspecting a CSV File with the head Command (Linux/macOS)

Before you start writing code to process a CSV file, it's often helpful to inspect it manually to get a sense of its structure and content. On Linux and macOS, you can use the head command to view the first few lines of a file:

```
head sales_data.csv
```

This will print the first 10 lines of the "sales_data.csv" file to the console, allowing you to see the header row, the delimiter, and the general format of the data.

In Summary: Embrace CSV as a Foundation, Understand Its Nuances

CSV files are a foundational data format for data analysis. Their simplicity and versatility make them a valuable tool for working with tabular data. By understanding the structure, variations, and limitations of CSV files, you can effectively leverage them in your Python projects.

9.2: Reading and Parsing Data with csv: Mastering the Art of Extraction

Now that we understand the structure and nuances of CSV files, let's dive into the heart of the matter: reading and parsing CSV data with Python's powerful csv module. This is where we unlock the potential of CSV files, extracting the raw data and transforming it into a format that we can analyze and manipulate.

The csv module provides a set of tools for reading and writing CSV files, handling the complexities of delimiters, quotes, and line endings. It's a fundamental skill for any data analyst working with Python.

The csv.reader Object: Your Key to Iterating Through CSV Data

The core of CSV parsing in Python is the csv.reader object. You create it by passing a file object (opened in text mode) to the csv.reader() function:

```
import csv

try:
```

```
    with open("sales_data.csv", "r", newline="",
encoding="utf-8") as file:
        reader = csv.reader(file)
        # ... process the CSV data ...
except FileNotFoundError:
    print("CSV file not found.")
```

Essential Elements:

- **import csv:** This line imports the csv module, making its functions and classes available.
- **with open(...) as file::** This opens the CSV file in text mode, ensuring it's properly closed afterward, even if errors occur. newline="" is crucial for handling line endings correctly across different operating systems. encoding="utf-8" is recommended for handling Unicode characters.
- **reader = csv.reader(file):** This creates a csv.reader object, which is an *iterator*. An iterator is an object that can be used to traverse a sequence of values, one at a time. In this case, the csv.reader object iterates over the rows in the CSV file.

Iterating Through Rows: One Line at a Time

The csv.reader object yields each row in the CSV file as a list of strings. You can iterate over these rows using a for loop:

```
    import csv

try:
    with open("sales_data.csv", "r", newline="",
encoding="utf-8") as file:
        reader = csv.reader(file)
        for row in reader:
            print(row)
except FileNotFoundError:
    print ("File not found")
except Exception as e:
    print (f"Error is {e}")
```

This code will print each row in the CSV file to the console as a list of strings.

Skipping the Header Row: Moving Beyond the Labels

Most CSV files have a header row that contains the names of the columns. You typically want to skip this row when processing the data. You can do this using the next() function:

```python
import csv

try:
    with open("sales_data.csv", "r", newline="",
encoding="utf-8") as file:
        reader = csv.reader(file)
        header = next(reader) #advance to the next line
        print(f"Header row: {header}") #show
        for row in reader:
            print(row) #all data after header
except FileNotFoundError:
    print("File not found")
except Exception as e:
    print (f"Error is {e}")
```

The next(reader) function retrieves the first row from the csv.reader object (which is the header row) and advances the iterator to the next row.

Customizing the Delimiter and Quote Character: Handling the Variations

CSV files don't always use commas as delimiters or double quotes as quote characters. The csv.reader() function allows you to customize these settings using the delimiter and quotechar parameters:

```python
import csv

try:
    with open("data_tab_separated.txt", "r", newline="",
encoding="utf-8") as file:
        reader = csv.reader(file, delimiter="\t",
quotechar="'")
        header = next(reader)
        print(f"Header row: {header}")

        for row in reader:
            print(row)

except FileNotFoundError:
    print ("File not found")
except Exception as e:
    print (f"Error is {e}")
```

In this example, we're reading a CSV file that uses tabs as delimiters and single quotes as quote characters.

The csv.DictReader Object: Accessing Data by Column Name

Instead of accessing data by column index, you can use the csv.DictReader object to access data by column name. This makes your code more readable and less prone to errors.

```
import csv

try:
    with open("sales_data.csv", "r", newline="",
encoding="utf-8") as file:
        reader = csv.DictReader(file) #creates a dict reader
object

        for row in reader:
            transaction_date = row["Transaction Date"] #get
the right value to each
            product_name = row["Product Name"]
            quantity_sold = row["Quantity Sold"]
            price = row["Price"]

            print(f"Date: {transaction_date}, Product:
{product_name}, Quantity: {quantity_sold}, Price: {price}")

except FileNotFoundError:
    print ("File not found")
except Exception as e:
    print (f"Error is {e}")
```

The csv.DictReader object reads the header row and uses it to create a dictionary for each subsequent row. You can then access the values in each row using the column names as keys.

Key Advantage: Using csv.DictReader makes your code more robust and easier to understand, as you don't have to rely on remembering the column indices.

Cleaning and Transforming Data: From Raw to Ready

CSV data often requires cleaning and transformation before it can be used for analysis. Common cleaning tasks include:

- **Removing Whitespace:** Use the strip() method to remove leading and trailing whitespace from values.
- **Converting Data Types:** Use int(), float(), and bool() to convert values to the appropriate data types.
- **Handling Missing Values:** Replace missing values with a default value (e.g., 0, "N/A", or None).
- **Normalizing Data:** Convert data to a consistent format (e.g., uppercase or lowercase, consistent date formats).

Let's add some cleaning and transformation steps to our example:

```python
import csv

try:
    with open("sales_data.csv", "r", newline="",
encoding="utf-8") as file:
        reader = csv.DictReader(file)

        for row in reader:
            #Clean it to avoid errors later
            transaction_date = row["Transaction
Date"].strip()
            product_name = row["Product Name"].strip()
            try:
                quantity_sold = int(row["Quantity
Sold"].strip())
                price = float(row["Price"].strip())
            except ValueError:
                print (f"Warning: Invalid data in row -
{row}")
                continue #move on to next row to avoid crash

            print(f"Date: {transaction_date}, Product:
{product_name}, Quantity: {quantity_sold}, Price: {price}")
except FileNotFoundError:
    print ("File not found")
except Exception as e:
    print (f"Error is {e}")
```

By adding these cleaning and transformation steps, you can ensure that your data is accurate and consistent.

In Summary: Become a CSV Parsing Pro

The csv module is a powerful and versatile tool for reading and parsing CSV files. By mastering the techniques presented in this section, you'll be able to confidently extract data from CSV files and transform it into a format that is ready for analysis.

9.3: Performing Basic Data Analysis: Weaving Data into Meaningful Stories

We've successfully extracted the raw data from our CSV file. Now comes the exciting part: performing data analysis. This is where we transform raw numbers into meaningful insights, uncover patterns, and tell stories with data.

Data analysis is not just about running calculations; it's about asking questions, exploring relationships, and drawing conclusions based on the evidence. It's a blend of technical skill and critical thinking.

The Analysis Process: A Step-by-Step Approach

While every data analysis project is unique, there's a general process that you can follow:

1. **Define Your Questions:** What are you trying to learn from the data? What questions do you want to answer? Without clear questions, you'll be wandering aimlessly through the data.
2. **Choose Appropriate Metrics:** Select the metrics that will help you answer your questions. These might include sums, averages, counts, percentages, or more complex statistics.
3. **Calculate the Metrics:** Use Python to calculate the metrics from your data.
4. **Interpret the Results:** What do the metrics tell you about your data? Are there any patterns or trends? Do the results surprise you?
5. **Communicate Your Findings:** Present your findings in a clear and concise way, using tables, charts, or summaries.

Applying the Process to Our Sales Data: A Case Study

Let's apply this process to our "sales_data.csv" file.

1. Define Your Questions:

Let's start with some questions:

- What is the total revenue for each product?
- Which product generates the most revenue?
- What is the average quantity sold per transaction?
- What is the total number of transactions?

2. Choose Appropriate Metrics:

To answer these questions, we'll need the following metrics:

- **Total Revenue per Product:** The sum of the revenue generated by each product.
- **Maximum Revenue:** The highest revenue generated by any single product.
- **Average Quantity Sold:** The total quantity sold divided by the total number of transactions.
- **Total Transactions:** The number of rows in the CSV file (excluding the header row).

3. Calculate the Metrics:

Let's use Python to calculate these metrics:

```python
import csv

product_revenue = {} #Dictionary of each products and revenue
generated
total_quantity = 0 #Total quanity of product
num_transactions = 0 #Number of transactions

try:
    with open("sales_data.csv", "r", newline="",
encoding="utf-8") as file:
        reader = csv.DictReader(file) #DictReader makes
columns accessible by name instead of index

        for row in reader:
            product_name = row["Product Name"].strip()
            quantity_sold = int(row["Quantity Sold"].strip())
            price = float(row["Price"].strip())

            revenue = quantity_sold * price

            if product_name in product_revenue:
                product_revenue[product_name] += revenue
```

```
        else:
            product_revenue[product_name] = revenue

        total_quantity += quantity_sold
        num_transactions += 1

except FileNotFoundError:
    print("Sales data file not found.")
except ValueError as e:
    print(f"Unable to convert value: {e}")
except Exception as e:
    print(f"File Processing Error: {e}")

average_quantity = total_quantity / num_transactions if
num_transactions > 0 else 0

#Determine best selling product
best_selling_product = max(product_revenue,
key=product_revenue.get) if product_revenue else "N/A"
max_revenue = product_revenue[best_selling_product] if
product_revenue else 0
```

Key Techniques:

- **Dictionary for Aggregation:** A dictionary is used to efficiently accumulate revenue for each product.
- **Total Accumulation:** The total quantity and number of transactions are accumulated within the loop.
- **Inline Conditional Expression:** The average quantity calculation uses an inline conditional to avoid division by zero.
- **Python Built-ins:** We use the built-in max() function to efficiently determine the best-selling product.
- **Data Conversion:** Handle data conversions as needed (e.g., int(), float()).

4. Interpret the Results:

Now that we've calculated the metrics, let's interpret the results.

- **Total Revenue per Product:** The product_revenue dictionary shows the total revenue generated by each product. This can help us identify our most popular and profitable products.
- **Best-Selling Product:** We will look at this as one of the key performance indicators to check which is performing the best.

- **Average Quantity Sold:** The average quantity sold per transaction can give us insights into the typical customer purchase.
- **Total Transactions:** The total number of transactions gives us a sense of the overall volume of sales.

5. Display the Results:

Finally, let's display the results in a clear and concise way:

```python
#show products and revenue

print ("\nRevenue Data")
for product, revenue in product_revenue.items():
    print(f"Product {product}: ${revenue:.2f}")

print(f"\nBest Selling Product: {best_selling_product}, ${max_revenue:.2f}")
print (f"Average Quantity Sold: {average_quantity:.2f}")
print (f"Total Number of Transactions: {num_transactions}")
```

This will print a summary of our findings to the console.

Beyond the Basics: Advanced Analysis Techniques

While this example demonstrates some basic data analysis techniques, there are many more advanced techniques that you can use to gain deeper insights from your data. These include:

- **Statistical Analysis:** Calculating measures of central tendency (mean, median, mode), measures of dispersion (variance, standard deviation), and correlations between variables.
- **Data Visualization:** Creating charts and graphs to visualize your data and identify patterns.
- **Machine Learning:** Using machine learning algorithms to build predictive models and identify hidden patterns in your data.

These advanced techniques are beyond the scope of this book, but they are worth exploring as you continue your data analysis journey.

In Summary: Transforming Data into Knowledge

Performing data analysis is about more than just running calculations; it's about asking questions, exploring relationships, and drawing conclusions. By following a structured process and using the right tools, you can transform raw data into valuable knowledge that can inform decisions and solve problems.

9.4: Displaying Results: Telling the Story of Your Data

You've crunched the numbers, performed the calculations, and uncovered some fascinating insights from your data. But your work isn't done yet! The final, and often most crucial, step is to *communicate* your findings to others.

Displaying results is not just about presenting the raw data; it's about telling a story. It's about crafting a narrative that is clear, concise, and compelling, and that resonates with your audience.

Think of it as being a journalist. You've gathered the facts, now you have to present them in a way that engages your readers and conveys the significance of your findings.

Knowing Your Audience: Tailoring Your Presentation

The best way to display your results depends heavily on your audience and the purpose of your analysis. Are you presenting to technical experts, business stakeholders, or the general public? What are they hoping to learn from your analysis?

Consider these factors:

- **Technical Expertise:** If your audience is technically savvy, you can use more complex terminology and visualizations. If your audience is non-technical, you'll need to simplify your language and use more intuitive representations.
- **Business Objectives:** What decisions will be made based on your analysis? Focus on presenting the information that is most relevant to those decisions.
- **Time Constraints:** How much time do you have to present your findings? If you have limited time, you'll need to focus on the key takeaways and avoid getting bogged down in details.

- **Presentation Medium:** Will your results be displayed in a console, in a report, in a presentation, or on a web page? The medium will influence the types of visualizations and formatting you can use.

Choosing the Right Format: The Medium is the Message

There are several ways to display your results, each with its own strengths and weaknesses:

- **Printing to the Console:** This is the simplest and most direct way to display results. It's suitable for quick explorations, debugging, and simple analyses.

  Best for: Quick feedback, debugging, or for programmatic processing.

- **Writing to a File (Text or CSV):** This allows you to store the results for later analysis or reporting. Writing to a CSV file makes it easy to import the data into a spreadsheet or database.

  Best for: Archiving data, feeding to external tools (spreadsheets, other programs).

- **Generating a Report (Plain Text or Formatted):** This allows you to create a more structured and professional presentation of your findings. You can use libraries like reportlab or pypandoc to create PDF reports.

  Best for: Formal documentation, presentations, sharing with non-technical audiences.

- **Creating Visualizations (Charts and Graphs):** This is often the most effective way to communicate complex data patterns and trends. Visualizations can make your findings more engaging, memorable, and persuasive.

  Best for: Identifying trends, presenting insights to diverse audiences, conveying complex information simply.

- **Building Interactive Dashboards (Web-Based):** This allows users to explore the data and drill down into details. Libraries like Plotly

Dash or Streamlit provide frameworks for creating interactive web dashboards.

Best for: Exploration, user interaction, real-time data monitoring.

For our To-Do List project, we can keep printing key information to the console:

```
    def display_product_revenue(product_revenue):
    """Displays the total revenue for each product."""
    print ("\nRevenue Data:")
    for product, revenue in product_revenue.items():
        print(f"Product {product}: ${revenue:.2f}")

# then, in your main analysis
display_product_revenue(product_revenue)
```

Tips for Effective Console Output: The Art of Brevity

Even with the simple output to the console, there are design decisions you can consider:

- **Use clear and concise labels:** Make sure it's obvious what each value represents.
- **Format numbers appropriately:** Use commas to separate thousands and limit the number of decimal places.
- **Use whitespace to improve readability:** Add blank lines and indentation to break up the output and make it easier to scan.
- **Highlight key findings:** Use bold text, color, or other formatting to draw attention to the most important results.

Let's improve the console output for our To-Do List project:

```
    #Existing code
if num_people > 0:
    average_age = total_age / num_people

    print("\n--- Analysis Summary ---") #Add Section Header,
easy to find
    print(f"Average Age: {average_age:.1f} years") # 1
decimal only
else:
    print ("No people found in file")
```

176

Communicating Uncertainty: Honesty in Data

It's important to be honest about the limitations of your data and the uncertainty associated with your findings. Avoid overstating your conclusions or making claims that are not supported by the evidence.

If you're working with a small sample size or if your data is incomplete, acknowledge these limitations and explain how they might affect your results.

In Summary: Present with Purpose, Communicate with Clarity

Displaying results is a crucial step in the data analysis process. By carefully considering your audience, choosing the right format, and communicating your findings clearly and honestly, you can transform raw data into valuable knowledge that can inform decisions and drive action.

9.5: Data Visualization: Turning Numbers into Art, Data into Understanding

While presenting your findings through text is important, often it is not enough. Humans are visual creatures. We process images far faster than text, making visual communication vital to understanding results.

Data visualization is the art and science of representing data graphically. It allows you to transform raw numbers into charts, graphs, and maps that reveal patterns, trends, and relationships that would be difficult to discern from tables of numbers alone.

Think of data visualization as painting a picture with data. You're using visual elements to tell a story, to communicate your findings in a way that is engaging, memorable, and persuasive.

It is key to tell data stories, so you are no longer just an analyst but a communicator.

Why Data Visualization Matters: Unlocking Insights and Driving Action

Data visualization is a powerful tool for several reasons:

- **Exploration:** Visualizations can help you explore your data and identify patterns that you might not otherwise see. They can spark new questions and lead to new discoveries.
- **Communication:** Visualizations can communicate complex information in a clear and concise way. They can help you explain your findings to others, even if they don't have a technical background.
- **Persuasion:** Visualizations can be more persuasive than tables of numbers. They can help you convince others of the validity of your findings and motivate them to take action.

Choosing the Right Chart: Matching the Visualization to the Data

The key to effective data visualization is to choose the right chart type for the type of data you're working with and the message you want to convey.

Here are some common chart types and their use cases:

- **Bar Charts:** Used to compare the values of different categories. *Ideal for:* Comparing sales revenue by product, website traffic by source, or customer satisfaction scores by region.
- **Line Charts:** Used to show trends over time. *Ideal for:* Tracking stock prices, website traffic, or temperature changes over time.
- **Scatter Plots:** Used to show the relationship between two variables. *Ideal for:* Identifying correlations between customer demographics and purchase behavior, or between advertising spend and sales revenue.
- **Pie Charts:** Used to show the proportion of different categories within a whole. *Ideal for:* Showing market share, budget allocation, or survey responses. *However use sparingly, as they can be difficult to read accurately.*
- **Histograms:** Used to show the distribution of a single variable. *Ideal for:* Understanding customer age, income levels, or website session durations.

The Matplotlib Library: Your Canvas for Data Art

Python offers several libraries for data visualization, but one of the most popular and versatile is Matplotlib. Matplotlib is a comprehensive library that provides a wide range of plotting functions, customization options, and output formats.

Let's explore some basic Matplotlib examples:

- **Importing Matplotlib:**

```
import matplotlib.pyplot as plt
```

  This line imports the pyplot module from the matplotlib library and assigns it the alias plt. This is the standard convention for working with Matplotlib.

- **Creating a Bar Chart:**

```
import matplotlib.pyplot as plt

products = ["A", "B", "C"]
revenue = [1000, 1500, 800]

plt.bar(products, revenue) #create bar chart with x-axis and y-axis
plt.xlabel("Products") # Label x axis
plt.ylabel("Revenue ($)") #label y axis
plt.title("Total Revenue by Product") #add title to the chart
plt.show()   # Display the chart
```

- **Creating a Line Chart:**

```
import matplotlib.pyplot as plt

dates = ["2023-01", "2023-02", "2023-03", "2023-04"]
sales = [500, 600, 750, 800]

plt.plot(dates, sales)  # Creates a line plot with dates on the x-axis and sales on the y-axis
plt.xlabel("Date")
plt.ylabel("Sales ($)")
plt.title("Sales Trend Over Time")
plt.show() #Open the plot display
```

- **Customizing Your Charts:**

Matplotlib offers a wide range of options for customizing your charts:

- o **Colors:** Use the color parameter to change the color of bars, lines, or points.
- o **Labels:** Use the xlabel(), ylabel(), and title() functions to add labels to your axes and chart.
- o **Legends:** Use the legend() function to add a legend to your chart.
- o **Markers:** Use the marker parameter to change the appearance of data points in a line chart.
- o **Line Styles:** Use the linestyle parameter to change the style of lines in a line chart.

Let's customize our bar chart:

```
import matplotlib.pyplot as plt

products = ["A", "B", "C"]
revenue = [1000, 1500, 800]

plt.bar(products, revenue, color="skyblue")  # Skyblue color
plt.xlabel("Product", fontsize=12) # Increase fontsize
plt.ylabel("Total Revenue ($)", fontsize=12)
plt.title("Total Revenue by Product", fontsize=14,
fontweight="bold") #Bolden Title
plt.show()
```

Beyond Matplotlib: Exploring Other Visualization Libraries

While Matplotlib is a powerful and versatile library, there are other data visualization libraries that you might want to explore:

- **Seaborn:** Seaborn builds on top of Matplotlib and provides a higher-level interface for creating more aesthetically pleasing and informative visualizations.
- **Plotly:** Plotly is a library for creating interactive, web-based visualizations.

Each library has its own strengths and weaknesses, so it's worth experimenting with different libraries to see which one best suits your needs.

Ethical Considerations: Visualizations Can Deceive

Data visualizations can be powerful tools for communication, but they can also be used to deceive. It's important to be aware of the potential for misuse and to use visualizations responsibly.

Here are some ethical considerations to keep in mind:

- **Avoid Misleading Scales:** Be careful when choosing the scale for your axes. A misleading scale can distort the perception of the data. Always make sure that your axes are clearly labeled and that the scale is appropriate for the data.
- **Don't Cherry-Pick Data:** Don't selectively present data that supports your argument while ignoring data that contradicts it. Be transparent about the limitations of your data and the uncertainty associated with your findings.
- **Avoid Distracting Visual Elements:** Focus on clarity and simplicity. Avoid using unnecessary visual elements that can distract from the data.

It is important that you do not use data visualization for nefarious purposes. The most important aspect of data is truth, not power.

In Summary: Data Visualization – The Art of Truthful Storytelling

Data visualization is a powerful tool for communicating your findings and insights. By choosing the right chart types, customizing your visualizations, and being mindful of ethical considerations, you can create compelling and informative visuals that engage your audience and drive action.

Chapter 10: Beyond the Basics: Your Python Adventure Continues

Congratulations! You've reached the end of our crash course. You've learned the fundamentals of Python programming, from variables and data types to control flow, functions, modules, and data analysis. You've even built a couple of practical projects.

But this is just the beginning of your Python journey. There's a vast world of knowledge and possibilities waiting to be explored. This chapter serves as your roadmap, pointing you in the direction of exciting new areas to explore and providing resources to help you along the way.

Think of this as the end of your apprenticeship and the beginning of your independent journey as a Python developer.

10.1: Navigating the Python Learning Landscape: Charting Your Course

You've reached the end of this crash course, but don't think for a moment that your Python education is complete. The truth is, learning Python is a lifelong journey. New libraries, frameworks, and techniques are constantly emerging, and there's always something new to discover.

The challenge isn't finding *information*; it's sifting through the *overabundance* of information to find the resources that are right for *you* at each stage of your development.

This section is your guide to navigating the Python learning landscape, helping you chart a course that is both effective and enjoyable.

The Official Python Documentation: Your Indispensable Companion

The official Python documentation is the single most important resource for any Python programmer. It's comprehensive, accurate, and well-organized, providing detailed information on all aspects of the language and its standard library.

URL: https://docs.python.org/3/

Why it's essential:

- **The Definitive Source:** It's written and maintained by the Python core developers, so it's the most authoritative source of information.
- **Comprehensive Coverage:** It covers all aspects of the language, from the syntax to the standard library modules.
- **Accurate and Up-to-Date:** It's regularly updated to reflect the latest changes in Python.
- **Well-Organized:** It's structured logically and easy to navigate, making it easy to find the information you need.

How to Use It Effectively:

- **Don't be intimidated:** The documentation can seem overwhelming at first, but don't be afraid to dive in. Start with the tutorials and gradually explore the more advanced sections.
- **Use the search function:** The search function is your best friend. Use it to quickly find information about specific functions, classes, or modules.
- **Read the examples:** The documentation includes many examples that demonstrate how to use different features of the language.
- **Contribute back:** If you find errors or areas for improvement, consider contributing back to the documentation.

Online Tutorials and Courses: Structured Learning Paths

Online tutorials and courses can provide a structured learning path, guiding you through the fundamentals of Python and helping you build a solid foundation.

- **Codecademy:** Offers interactive Python courses that are great for beginners. Their interactive format makes learning engaging and hands-on.
  - *Why it's good:* Interactive, beginner-friendly, covers the basics well.
- **Coursera/edX:** Offer university-level Python courses from top institutions. These courses are more rigorous and in-depth than most other online resources.
  - *Why they're good:* High-quality content, structured learning path, certificates of completion.

- **Udemy:** Offers a wide variety of Python courses, both free and paid. The quality of Udemy courses can vary, so it's important to read reviews before enrolling.
  - *Why it's good:* Wide variety of topics, affordable prices, self-paced learning.

Tips for Choosing a Course:

- **Read Reviews:** Check what other students say about the course and the instructor.
- **Check the Syllabus:** Make sure the course covers the topics you're interested in.
- **Consider Your Learning Style:** Do you prefer interactive learning, video lectures, or reading text? Choose a course that matches your learning style.
- **Start with Free Courses:** Many platforms offer free introductory courses. Use these to get a feel for the platform and the instructor before committing to a paid course.

Books: In-Depth Exploration and Reference

Books provide a more in-depth and comprehensive exploration of Python than most online resources. They're also great for reference, allowing you to quickly look up information when you need it.

Recommendations depend on your specific areas of interest:

- *Effective Python by Brett Slatkin*: A fantastic book on Python best practices.
- *Python Crash Course by Eric Matthes*: A beginner-friendly guide that covers the fundamentals of Python and helps you build real-world projects.
- *Automate the Boring Stuff with Python by Al Sweigart*: A practical guide to using Python to automate common tasks.
- *Fluent Python by Luciano Ramalho*: A deep dive into the more advanced and idiomatic aspects of Python. (For intermediate to advanced learners)

Tips for Choosing a Book:

- **Read Reviews:** See what other readers say about the book.

- **Check the Table of Contents:** Make sure the book covers the topics you're interested in.
- **Read Sample Chapters:** Many books offer sample chapters online. Use these to get a feel for the author's writing style and the book's level of difficulty.
- **Consider Your Skill Level:** Choose a book that is appropriate for your current skill level.

Online Communities: Connect, Learn, and Contribute

The Python community is a vibrant and welcoming group of developers, users, and enthusiasts. Engaging with the community is a great way to learn new skills, get help with problems, and connect with other Pythonistas.

- **Stack Overflow:** A question-and-answer website for programmers. It's a great place to ask questions and find solutions to common problems.
  - *Tip: Search before you ask!* Chances are, someone has already asked your question.
- **Reddit:** The r/python subreddit is a great place to discuss Python news, share resources, and ask questions.
  - *Tip: Be respectful and follow the subreddit rules.*
- **Python Discord Server:** Connect with other Python developers in real time on the Python Discord server. This is a great place to get quick help with problems or just chat about Python.
- **Python Mailing Lists:** Participate in Python mailing lists to discuss specific topics or get involved in the development of Python itself.

Tips for Engaging with Online Communities:

- **Be Respectful:** Treat others with respect, even if you disagree with them.
- **Be Specific:** When asking questions, provide as much detail as possible.
- **Show Effort:** Demonstrate that you've tried to solve the problem yourself before asking for help.
- **Contribute Back:** Share your knowledge and experience with others.

The Most Important Skill: Learning How to Learn

In the fast-paced world of technology, the ability to learn quickly and effectively is more important than ever. Develop your skills in:

- **Identifying Your Learning Style:** What methods work best for you?
- **Breaking Down Complex Topics:** How do you decompose a huge challenge into smaller, actionable steps?
- **Seeking and Evaluating Information:** How do you separate good advice from bad?
- **Practicing Deliberately:** How can you make your practice time most effective?

In Summary: A Journey of Continuous Learning

The resources listed in this section are just a starting point. There's a vast amount of information available online and in print. The key is to be proactive, to seek out the resources that are right for you, and to never stop learning. As you continue your Python journey, remember to be curious, to be persistent, and to have fun!

10.2: Object-Oriented Programming: A New Way to Organize Your Code

Throughout this crash course, we've primarily used a *procedural* programming style. That is, we have defined functions that operate on data. While this approach works well for small to medium-sized projects, it can become difficult to manage as your code grows larger and more complex.

That's where Object-Oriented Programming (OOP) comes in. OOP is a powerful paradigm that allows you to organize your code into reusable objects that encapsulate data and behavior. It's a way of thinking about code that can lead to more modular, maintainable, and scalable applications.

Think of OOP as moving from individual tools to building entire *machines* that have specific jobs.

Why OOP Matters: Taming Complexity and Promoting Reusability

OOP addresses several key challenges in software development:

- **Complexity Management:** OOP allows you to break down complex problems into smaller, more manageable pieces. Each object represents a distinct entity in your system, making it easier to reason about the overall behavior.

- **Code Reusability:** OOP promotes code reuse through inheritance and polymorphism. You can create new classes based on existing classes, inheriting their attributes and methods.
- **Data Encapsulation:** OOP allows you to protect your data from accidental modification by encapsulating it within objects. This helps to ensure data integrity.
- **Modularity:** OOP promotes modularity, making it easier to maintain and extend your code. You can change the implementation of one object without affecting other parts of the system.

Core Concepts of OOP: Building Blocks of Object-Oriented Code

Let's explore the key concepts of OOP:

- **Classes: The Blueprint for Objects**

  A class is a blueprint or template for creating objects. It defines the attributes (data) and methods (behavior) that objects of that class will have.

  Consider an analogy: The class is like the blueprint for a house. It specifies the number of rooms, the size of the rooms, and the materials that will be used to build the house.

  Example:

  ```
  class Dog: #This line is the class declaration
  """Represents a dog."""

  def __init__(self, name, breed): # __init__ (Constructor)
      """Initializes a Dog object."""
      self.name = name
      self.breed = breed

  def bark(self):   #Methods
      """Makes the dog bark."""
      print("Woof!")
  ```

  Essential: Notice the self parameter in the methods. This refers to the *instance* of the class. Methods always need to know which instance they are operating on.

- **Objects: Instances of a Class**

An object is a specific instance of a class. It's a concrete realization of the blueprint.

Continuing our house analogy, an object is like a specific house that was built according to the blueprint. It has its own unique address, its own paint color, and its own set of occupants.

Example:

```
my_dog = Dog("Buddy", "Golden Retriever") #make object
of dog type
print(my_dog.name)    # Output: Buddy
print(my_dog.breed)   # Output: Golden Retriever
my_dog.bark() #output Woof!
```

- **Attributes: Describing the Object**

  Attributes are the data associated with an object. They represent the object's state or characteristics.

  In our Dog class, name and breed are attributes. Each Dog object has its own unique values for these attributes.

- **Methods: Object Behaviors**

  Methods are functions that are associated with an object. They define the object's behavior, what it *can do*.

  In our Dog class, bark() is a method. It defines the action that a Dog object can perform.

- **Encapsulation: Bundling Data and Behavior**

  Encapsulation is the process of bundling data (attributes) and methods together into a single unit (the object). This helps to protect the data from accidental modification and makes the code more modular.

  In our Dog class, the name, breed, and bark() method are all encapsulated within the Dog object. This means that you can only access or modify the data through the object's methods.

- **Inheritance: Building on Existing Classes**

   Inheritance allows you to create new classes based on existing classes, inheriting their attributes and methods. This promotes code reuse and makes it easier to create a hierarchy of classes.

   Example:

```python
class Poodle(Dog): #Poodle inherits from the Dog class
    """Represents a Poodle."""

    def __init__(self, name): #Calling super() is to invoke
the Dog parent class, and create a new class that inherits
from it.
        super().__init__(name, "Poodle")  # Calls the Dog
class's constructor
    def do_trick(self): #Add another function specific to
Poodle
        print(f"{self.name} did a trick!")
my_poodle = Poodle("Fifi") #make object of Poodle type
my_poodle.bark() #Poodle can bark, inherited from Dog
my_poodle.do_trick()#Poodle can also do trick
```

   The Poodle class inherits the name, breed, and bark() method from the Dog class. It also adds a new method, do_trick().

- **Polymorphism: Different Objects, Same Interface**

   Polymorphism is the ability of objects of different classes to respond to the same method call in different ways. This allows you to write code that can work with objects of different types without knowing their specific class.

   Let's say you have a list of animal objects, some of which are dogs and some of which are cats. You can call the make_sound() method on each object, and each object will respond in its own way:

```python
class Cat:
    def __init__(self, name):
        self.name = name
    def make_sound(self):
        print("Meow!")

animals = [Dog("Buddy", "Golden Retriever"), Cat("Whiskers")]
```

```
for animal in animals:
    animal.make_sound()   # Output: Woof! Meow!
```

From Procedural to Object-Oriented: A Shift in Perspective

Moving from procedural programming to OOP requires a shift in perspective. Instead of thinking about functions that operate on data, you need to think about objects that encapsulate data and behavior. It's about modeling the real world in your code.

In Summary: Embrace OOP for Scalable and Maintainable Code

Object-Oriented Programming is a powerful tool for building complex and scalable applications. By mastering the key concepts of OOP, you'll be able to write code that is more modular, maintainable, and reusable.

10.3: Web Development: From Local Code to Global Reach

We've learned how to build command-line tools and analyze data. Now, let's explore how to take your Python skills to the next level and build applications that can be accessed by anyone in the world through a web browser.

Web development is the process of creating applications that run on web servers and are accessed by users through web browsers. It's a vast and complex field, but Python, with frameworks like Flask and FastAPI, makes it surprisingly accessible.

Think of web development as building a bridge between your code and the internet, allowing users from all over the world to interact with your creations.

The Core Components of Web Development: A Bird's-Eye View

Web development involves several key components:

1. **The Front-End (What the User Sees):** This is the part of the application that the user interacts with directly. It's built using HTML, CSS, and JavaScript.

- HTML (HyperText Markup Language): Defines the structure and content of web pages (e.g., headings, paragraphs, images, links).
- CSS (Cascading Style Sheets): Styles the appearance of web pages (e.g., colors, fonts, layout).
- JavaScript: Adds interactivity to web pages (e.g., animations, form validation, dynamic content).

2. **The Back-End (What Powers the Application):** This is the part of the application that runs on the server and handles the logic, data storage, and communication with the front-end. Python, with frameworks like Flask and FastAPI, is often used for back-end development.

3. **The Web Server:** A software that listens for requests from web browsers and serves the appropriate files (HTML, CSS, JavaScript, images, etc.). Common web servers include Apache, Nginx, and Gunicorn.

4. **The Database:** A system for storing and retrieving data (e.g., user accounts, product information, blog posts). Common databases include PostgreSQL, MySQL, and MongoDB.

In essence, the front-end is the face of your application, while the back-end is the brain and the database is the memory.

Python Web Frameworks: Your Tools for Building Web Applications

Python offers several web frameworks that simplify the process of building web applications. These frameworks provide pre-built components, tools, and conventions that help you structure your code, handle requests, and generate responses.

Two popular Python web frameworks are:

- **Flask: The Microframework**

  Flask is a lightweight and flexible framework that is easy to learn and use. It's often referred to as a "microframework" because it provides only the essential tools for building web applications, leaving you with the freedom to choose other components as needed.

  Flask is well-suited for small to medium-sized applications, such as personal websites, blogs, and simple APIs.

- **FastAPI: The Modern, High-Performance Framework**

  FastAPI is a modern, high-performance framework for building APIs (Application Programming Interfaces). It's designed for building fast and scalable web applications, and it includes features like automatic data validation, API documentation, and support for asynchronous programming.

  FastAPI is a good choice for building complex APIs and web applications that require high performance.

A Glimpse into Flask: A Simple "Hello, World" Application

Let's create a simple "Hello, World" application using Flask:

1. **Install Flask:**

   ```
   pip install Flask
   ```

2. **Create a Python File (app.py):**

   ```python
   from flask import Flask

   app = Flask(__name__)

   @app.route("/") #add a route which connects to the view
   function
   def hello_world(): #view function
       return "<p>Hello, World!</p>" #string that returns to
   browser

   if __name__ == '__main__': #ensures flask web server only run
   when the script is run directly
       app.run(debug=True) #runs flask application, change debug
   = False when deploying
   ```

3. **Run the Application:**

   ```
   python app.py
   ```

4. **Open Your Web Browser:**

Navigate to http://127.0.0.1:5000/ in your web browser. You should see the message "Hello, World!" displayed on the page.

Let's break this code down:

- **from flask import Flask:** Imports the Flask class from the flask module.
- **app = Flask(__name__):** Creates a Flask application object. The __name__ variable is a special Python variable that represents the name of the current module.
- **@app.route("/"):** This is a decorator that associates the hello_world() function with the root URL ("/"). When a user visits the root URL, Flask will call the hello_world() function and return its value as the response.
- **def hello_world()::** This is a function that returns the string "Hello, World!". This string will be displayed in the web browser.
- **if __name__ == '__main__'::** The if statement will check if the current file is being run directly.
- **app.run(debug=True):** Runs the Flask application in debug mode. Debug mode provides helpful error messages and automatically reloads the server when you make changes to your code. *Make sure to set debug=False when you deploy your application to production!*

The World of Web Development Awaits

This is just a taste of what's possible with web development using Python. With Flask or FastAPI, you can build complex web applications, APIs, and microservices that power the modern web.

To go further, you'll need to learn about:

- **Templates:** Rendering dynamic HTML content.
- **Forms:** Handling user input.
- **Databases:** Storing and retrieving data.
- **Authentication:** Securing your application.
- **Deployment:** Making your application accessible to the world.

In Summary: From Code to the Cloud

Web development opens up a whole new world of possibilities for your Python skills. By learning a web framework like Flask or FastAPI, you can build interactive web applications and share your creations with the world.

10.4: Data Science Awaits: NumPy and Pandas- Your Keys to Unlocking Data's Secrets

We've touched on basic file handling and even performed some rudimentary data analysis. But to truly unlock the power of data, you need to arm yourself with the right tools. In the Python world, those tools are, first and foremost, NumPy and Pandas.

Data science is an interdisciplinary field that uses scientific methods, processes, algorithms, and systems to extract knowledge and insights from structured and unstructured data. It is an enormous field that is rapidly changing the world around us.

NumPy and Pandas are two fundamental libraries that form the backbone of the Python data science ecosystem. They provide powerful tools for working with numerical data, manipulating data structures, and performing statistical analysis. Mastering these libraries is essential for anyone who wants to pursue a career in data science or simply gain a deeper understanding of the data that surrounds us.

Think of NumPy and Pandas as giving you superhuman abilities to manipulate, analyze, and understand enormous datasets.

NumPy: The Foundation for Numerical Computing

NumPy (Numerical Python) is the foundation for numerical computing in Python. It provides support for arrays, matrices, and a wide range of mathematical functions. NumPy arrays are similar to Python lists, but they are much more efficient for numerical operations.

Key Features and Real-World Use cases:

- **Arrays:** NumPy arrays are multi-dimensional arrays that can store numerical data of the same type. They are much more efficient than Python lists for numerical operations.
- **Mathematical Functions:** NumPy provides a wide range of mathematical functions, such as trigonometric functions, logarithmic functions, and statistical functions.
- **Linear Algebra:** NumPy provides support for linear algebra operations, such as matrix multiplication, eigenvalue decomposition, and solving linear systems.

- **Random Number Generation:** NumPy provides functions for generating random numbers from various distributions.

Let's see an example of how to use NumPy to calculate the mean and standard deviation of a dataset:

```
import numpy as np

data = [1, 2, 3, 4, 5, 6, 7, 8, 9, 10]

#Calculate array using NumPy
data_array = np.array(data)

mean = np.mean(data_array)
std_dev = np.std(data_array)

print(f"Mean: {mean}")
print(f"Standard Deviation: {std_dev}")
```

Pandas: Data Analysis and Manipulation Made Easy

Pandas is a library for data analysis and manipulation. It provides data structures like DataFrames and Series that make it easy to work with tabular data. Pandas is built on top of NumPy, so it inherits NumPy's performance and efficiency.

Key Features and Real-World Use cases:

- **DataFrames:** DataFrames are two-dimensional tables with labeled rows and columns. They are similar to spreadsheets or SQL tables.
- **Series:** Series are one-dimensional arrays with labeled indices. They can be thought of as columns in a DataFrame.
- **Data Cleaning:** Pandas provides powerful tools for cleaning and transforming data, such as handling missing values, filtering rows, and merging datasets.
- **Data Analysis:** Pandas provides functions for performing a wide range of data analysis tasks, such as calculating summary statistics, grouping data, and creating pivot tables.

Let's see an example of how to use Pandas to read a CSV file, clean the data, and calculate the average price:

```
import pandas as pd
```

```
try:
    #Read csv using pandas
    df = pd.read_csv("sales_data.csv")
    #clean column names to prevent errors
    df.columns = df.columns.str.replace(' ', '')

    df['Price'] = pd.to_numeric(df['Price'], errors='coerce')
#If conversion fails replace with NaN

    average_price = df['Price'].mean()

    print(f"Average Price: ${average_price:.2f}")

except FileNotFoundError as e:
    print(f"Error with file: {e}")
except Exception as e:
    print (f"General processing error: {e}")
```

The power of Pandas shows in its easy handling of the CSVs, which are difficult to manage with Python alone.

The Data Science Workflow: From Data to Insights

Data science projects typically follow a well-defined workflow:

1. **Data Acquisition:** Gathering data from various sources (e.g., CSV files, databases, web APIs).
2. **Data Cleaning:** Preparing the data for analysis by handling missing values, correcting errors, and transforming data types.
3. **Data Exploration:** Exploring the data, identifying patterns, and formulating hypotheses.
4. **Data Analysis:** Applying statistical techniques and machine learning algorithms to test hypotheses and build predictive models.
5. **Data Visualization:** Creating charts and graphs to communicate your findings.
6. **Communication and Storytelling:** Presenting your findings in a clear and concise way to stakeholders.

Beyond NumPy and Pandas: Expanding Your Data Science Toolkit

While NumPy and Pandas are essential, there are many other data science libraries that you might want to explore:

- **Scikit-learn:** A comprehensive library for machine learning.
- **Matplotlib:** A library for creating static, interactive, and animated visualizations in Python.
- **Seaborn:** A higher-level library that builds on top of Matplotlib and provides a more user-friendly interface for creating statistical visualizations.
- **Statsmodels:** A library for statistical modeling and inference.

The Call to Action: Embark on Your Data Science Journey

Learning data science is a challenging but rewarding endeavor. It requires a combination of technical skills, analytical thinking, and creativity. But with the right tools and resources, anyone can learn to extract valuable insights from data.

I encourage you to take the first step and start exploring NumPy and Pandas. There are countless online tutorials, courses, and books that can help you get started. And remember, the best way to learn is by doing. Find a dataset that interests you and start experimenting!

In Summary: Data Science: The Future is Data-Driven

Data science is transforming the world around us, and Python is at the forefront of this revolution. By mastering NumPy and Pandas, you can unlock the power of data and contribute to this exciting and rapidly growing field.

10.5: Contributing to the Python Community: Paying It Forward

You've learned a lot in this crash course, and you're now equipped with the fundamentals of Python programming. But the journey doesn't end here! One of the most rewarding aspects of being a Python developer is the opportunity to contribute back to the community that has given so much to us.

The Python community is a vibrant and welcoming group of developers, users, and enthusiasts from all over the world. It's a place where you can learn from others, share your knowledge, and collaborate on projects that make a difference.

What makes a language truly special? The community that builds up around it.

Contributing to the Python community is not just about giving back; it's also about:

- **Learning New Skills:** You'll learn new programming techniques, design patterns, and problem-solving strategies.
- **Building Your Network:** You'll connect with other Python developers from all over the world.
- **Making a Difference:** You'll contribute to projects that are used by millions of people.
- **Boosting Your Career:** Contributing to open-source projects can enhance your resume and demonstrate your skills to potential employers.

Beyond Code: Diverse Ways to Contribute

The beautiful thing about contributing to an open-source community is that not everyone is a code expert. You can contribute regardless of your skill levels.

There are many ways to contribute to the Python community, even if you're not a seasoned programmer:

- **Write Documentation:** Good documentation is essential for any project. You can help by writing tutorials, improving existing documentation, or translating documentation into other languages.
- **Report Bugs:** When you find a bug in a Python library or framework, report it to the developers. Be as specific as possible about how to reproduce the bug.
- **Answer Questions on Stack Overflow:** Help other Python developers by answering their questions on Stack Overflow.
- **Write Blog Posts or Tutorials:** Share your knowledge and experience by writing blog posts or tutorials about Python.
- **Present at Conferences or Meetups:** Share your expertise by presenting at conferences or meetups.
- **Organize Python Events:** Organize local Python meetups or workshops.
- **Promote Python:** Advocate for Python by giving talks, writing articles, or simply sharing your enthusiasm for the language with others.

- **Code Review**: Review code contributions made by others and help them to correct issues that would cause runtime issues.
- **Be Welcoming and Inclusive:** Help to create a welcoming and inclusive environment for all Python developers. This means being respectful of others, being patient with beginners, and actively working to combat bias and discrimination.

Contributing to Open-Source Projects: A Deeper Dive

Contributing to open-source projects can seem intimidating at first, but it's actually a very rewarding experience. Here are some tips for getting started:

1. **Find a Project You're Passionate About:** Choose a project that you're interested in and that you use regularly. This will make it easier to stay motivated and to contribute meaningfully.
2. **Start Small:** Don't try to tackle a huge feature or fix a complex bug right away. Start with small tasks, such as fixing typos, improving documentation, or writing unit tests.
3. **Read the Contribution Guidelines:** Most open-source projects have contribution guidelines that outline how to submit code, report bugs, and participate in discussions. Be sure to read these guidelines carefully before making any contributions.
4. **Fork the Repository:** To contribute code, you'll need to fork the repository on GitHub (or another code hosting platform). This creates a copy of the repository in your own account.
5. **Create a Branch:** Create a new branch in your forked repository for your changes. This keeps your changes separate from the main codebase.
6. **Make Your Changes:** Make your code changes, following the project's coding style and guidelines.
7. **Test Your Changes:** Make sure that your changes work correctly and don't introduce any new bugs.
8. **Submit a Pull Request:** Once you're satisfied with your changes, submit a pull request (PR) to the main repository. This proposes your changes to the project maintainers.
9. **Respond to Feedback:** Be prepared to respond to feedback from the project maintainers. They might ask you to make changes to your code or documentation.
10. **Be Patient:** Open-source projects are often run by volunteers, so it might take some time for your pull request to be reviewed and merged.

A Personal Invitation: Join the Community!

I encourage you to actively participate in this vibrant world. It's a place where you can learn, grow, and make a difference. By sharing your knowledge, contributing to open-source projects, and helping others, you'll not only improve your own skills but also make a positive impact on the Python community and the world at large.

In Summary: Code is a Shared Endeavor

Your journey with Python does not have to be a solitary affair. Code is about problem solving, and solving problems can be easier and more rewarding with a supportive community! So, embrace the Python community, give back in whatever way you can, and help make it an even better place for everyone.

Appendix

Appendix A: Common Errors and Debugging: Your Troubleshooting Guide

Even the most experienced programmers encounter errors from time to time. Errors are a natural part of the programming process. The key is not to avoid errors altogether (that's impossible!), but to learn how to understand them, diagnose them, and fix them efficiently.

This appendix serves as your troubleshooting guide, providing information on common Python errors and how to debug them.

1. SyntaxError: Invalid Syntax

This is one of the most common errors, and it usually indicates that you've made a mistake in the syntax of your code (e.g., a missing colon, a mismatched parenthesis, or an invalid keyword).

Example:

```
if x > 5
print("x is greater than 5") # Missing colon
```

Solution: Carefully review the line of code that the error message points to and check for any syntax errors. Make sure you have the correct punctuation, indentation, and keywords. A code editor with syntax highlighting can greatly help.

2. NameError: Name 'variable_name' is not defined

This error occurs when you try to use a variable that hasn't been assigned a value.

Example:

```
print(y) # y has not been defined yet.
y = 10
```

Solution: Make sure that you define all variables before using them. Check for typos in variable names.

3. TypeError: Unsupported operand type(s) for +: 'int' and 'str'

This error occurs when you try to perform an operation on incompatible data types.

Example:

```
age = 30
name = "Alice"
print(age + name) #Unable to add an integer to a string
```

Solution: Make sure that you're using the correct data types for your operations. Use type conversion functions (e.g., int(), str(), float()) to convert values to the appropriate types.

4. IndexError: List index out of range

This error occurs when you try to access an element in a list using an index that is outside of the valid range.

Example:

```
my_list = [1, 2, 3]
print(my_list[3]) #Index 3 does not exist, as indexes start at 0
```

Solution: Make sure that you're using valid indices when accessing list elements. Remember that list indices start at 0 and end at len(list) - 1. Use len() to check the length of the list.

5. KeyError: 'key_name'

This error occurs when you try to access a key in a dictionary that doesn't exist.

Example:

```
my_dict = {"name": "Alice", "age": 30}
```

```
print(my_dict["city"]) #key value city does not exist.
```

Solution: Make sure that the key exists in the dictionary before trying to access it. Use the get() method to access dictionary values safely, or test with 'key' in my_dict.

6. FileNotFoundError: [Errno 2] No such file or directory: 'file.txt'

This error occurs when you try to open a file that doesn't exist.

Example:

```
file = open("nonexistent_file.txt", "r") #the file
doesn't exist
```

Solution: Make sure that the file exists in the specified location. Check for typos in the file name. Use a try-except block to handle the FileNotFoundError gracefully.

7. IndentationError: Expected an indented block

This error occurs when you're missing an indented block after a statement that requires one (e.g., an if statement, a for loop, a function definition).

Example:

```
if True:
print("Hello") #missing indentation for block in if statement
```

Solution: Make sure that you indent the code inside the block correctly. Use 4 spaces for indentation.

General Debugging Tips: Your Toolkit for Solving Problems

In addition to understanding common errors, it's also important to have a set of general debugging skills that you can use to solve any problem:

- **Read the Error Message Carefully:** The error message often contains valuable information about what went wrong and where the error occurred. Read it carefully and try to understand what it's telling you.

- **Use print() Statements:** Use print() statements to display the values of variables, the flow of execution, and other information that can help you understand what's happening in your code.
- **Use a Debugger:** A debugger is a tool that allows you to step through your code line by line, inspect variables, and set breakpoints. This can be invaluable for tracking down complex bugs. Most IDEs have a debugger.
- **Simplify the Problem:** If you're having trouble debugging a complex piece of code, try to simplify it by removing unnecessary parts. This can help you isolate the source of the error.
- **Search Online:** Search the web for the error message or a description of the problem. Chances are, someone else has encountered the same issue and has posted a solution online.
- **Ask for Help:** Don't be afraid to ask for help from other developers or on online forums. Sometimes, a fresh pair of eyes can spot a problem that you've been overlooking.

Debugging Mindset: Embrace the Challenge

Debugging can be frustrating, but it's also an essential part of the programming process. Embrace the challenge, be patient, and remember that every bug you fix makes you a better programmer.

End of Appendix A

Appendix B: Python Style Guide (PEP 8 Summary)

The purpose of PEP 8 is to have a consistent set of standards so the code has a consistent layout. It is not meant to be dogmatic or inflexible. Try to use your best judgement.

- **Indentation:** Use 4 spaces for indentation. Never use tabs.
- **Line Length:** Limit lines to a maximum of 79 characters. For flowing long blocks of text, lines should be limited to 72 characters.
- **Blank Lines:**
  - Surround top-level function and class definitions with two blank lines.
  - Method definitions inside a class are surrounded by a single blank line.

- Use blank lines sparingly inside functions to separate logical sections of code.
- **Imports:**
  - Imports should be at the top of the file, after any module comments and docstrings, and before global or constants declarations.
  - Imports should be grouped in the following order: standard library imports, related third party imports, local application/library specific imports. Put a blank line between each group of imports.
- **Whitespace:**
  - Surround operators and assignments with a single space on either side (except for exponentiation).
  - Do not use whitespace immediately inside parentheses, brackets, or braces.
  - Do not use excessive whitespace to align code.
- **Naming Conventions:**
  - Use snake_case for variable names, function names, and module names.
  - Use PascalCase for class names.
  - Use UPPER_CASE for constants.
- **Comments:**
  - Write clear and concise comments that explain the *purpose* of the code, not just what it does.
  - Use docstrings to document functions, classes, and modules.

www.ingramcontent.com/pod-product-compliance
Lightning Source LLC
LaVergne TN
LVHW081525050326
832903LV00025B/1631